# Yesterday's Children:

## Growing up Assyrian in Persia

By Elizabeth Yoel Campbell
Edited by Carolyn Karam-Barkley

Text © Elizabeth Yoel Campbell and Carolyn Karam-Barkley

Cover Design and Layout by Jennifer W. Monroe

ISBN # 978-1-60145-277-1

# Dedication

*To the memory of my Parents,*
*YOEL & SHUSHAN YOSEPH*
*and to the Assyrian and Armenian Victims*
*of Turko-Kurdish Massacres*
*during World War One*

# forward

*Yesterday's Children* is the true story of an Assyrian family who in the colorful, if dangerous, years of the early twentieth century lived in the very heart of Shiite Islam in a far flung corner of the Persian Empire. In explanation of who we were and where our people originated I have added some general Assyrian history. This historical view is not a scholarly thesis, therefore, if the reader is looking for a well researched historical document there are books available on the subject provided by historians, archeologists and professional travelers of the nineteenth and twentieth centuries.

A few years ago when, on the spur of the moment in answer to an advertisement by our local Neighborhood Learning House, I joined a Creative Writing class I had no idea that I would soon be on my way to writing a book. From the start when I first read to the class what eventually became the first chapter of *Yesterday's Children*, there was so much interest and enthusiasm that I knew, for me, there would be no turning back. The list of questions they fired at me grew and grew: What was Persia like three-quarters of a century ago? What were conditions like for veiled Muslim women? What about their religion? Tell us more about the Assyrians, tell us about your schools, the kinds of games you used to play, your lifestyle, the standard of living, etc. Also, please tell us more about the shahs. People were absolutely fascinated by Persia and its shahs, but seemed to have an aversion to Iran and Iranians. In consequence, and in answer to all those questions, my story grew haphazardly without any particular plan, though I think I always knew just how I would bring the story to a close.

I was shocked, and somewhat deflated, when I realized that most of the class had either not heard about ancient Assyria and Assyrians, or they thought of us as a barbarian, and now extinct, race belonging in the pages of musty archives that no one bothered to read. From then on I had an ambition, a burning desire to enlighten them as to our place in history and our people's contribution to civilization. When it came to writing about the fall of Atra (our autonomous homeland in Turkey) and of Baz, my father's clan, I could only approach the subject in the way I had felt and understood events as a child. In my most susceptible and impressionable years these stories were told and retold to us until, for me, they became an almost personal experience. *Yesterday's Children* should be read with this in mind and allowances made for the way the story is told, from a child's point of view.

I owe a debt of gratitude to Robyn Hillard, published poet, writer, and my teacher for her tireless efforts on behalf of all her students, especially myself. Without her encouragement, sacrifice of hours of her free time, and her implicit belief in my ability to finish what I started, *Yesterday's Children* would never have been written. Thanks are also due to my brother William Yoel of Cleveland, Ohio, who was always ready to refresh my memory and supply me with information which I lacked.

Last, but not least, many thanks to Jenny Poon, Director of Neighborhood Learning House, for making the facilities available to the community, and for the congenial atmosphere she has created where young and old, teacher and student can meet on equal footing to share knowledge.

I would like to pay tribute to the Muslim inhabitants of Maragha during the WWI era. Throughout the book I have written kindly and affectionately about my corner of Persia, as it was known then, and of Persians, though I know that many Christians who lived through the frenzied jihads of those years would disagree with these sentiments. The Christian experience was quite different in my neck of the woods. Several powerful and fanatical delegations came to Maragha to incite the locals to rise up against the Christians, and to wipe out the unbelievers amongst them. But always, with the leadership of the Ayatollah and the Governor, they refused to go down that path, and such delegations were politely, but firmly shown to the city gates. Christian refugees kept pouring into the city, and those who could not be accommodated inside were given protection outside the city walls. It is certain that without their compassion and courage in the face of fanatical religious and Ottoman political pressure, history would have been written differently. It is estimated that 750,000 Assyrians, 1,500,000 Armenians, and countless other Christian groups were put to death by the Ottoman Turks and Kurds. Many more thousands of Christian lives would have been lost had it not been for the leadership of the Ayatollah and Governor, including the lives of my entire family.

# Editor's Note

Elizabeth Yoel Campbell began writing **Yesterday's Children** in her late 70's as a series of exercises for a creative writing class. She so compelled her classmates with accounts of early 20th century life in Azerbaijan, Persia, that they demanded more and more episodes of her tales. Just as Scheherazade had done before her, once the stories began pouring out, she knew there could be no turning back. **Yesterday's Children** was not born out of a conscious intention to write a book but out of a need to recount and preserve family stories that had been told and re-told for generations.

For Elizabeth Yoel Campbell, the outpouring of these personal memories is a gift to her family, and also of cultural value to all Assyrians living in diaspora in the Western world. While migration from ancestral homelands offered greater opportunities for political, religious, and economic freedom, immigrants risked losing their social order, language, and stories within the melting pot nations they would enter, thus disconnecting them from their ancestral roots. The following stories come together to create a snapshot of the time when "homeland" was just beginning to unravel for the Assyrians of the Middle East.

**Yesterday's Children** acquaints us with a seldom heard recent history of Assyrians in the Middle East, and the revelation that they continue to exist there and elsewhere, carrying on an unbroken chain of survival since ancient times. This is all the more remarkable since the Assyrian Empire fell as an official state in 612B.C. In fact, the Assyrian New Year, *Kha B'Nissan*, which is observed each year on April 1st, marked the year 6755 on April 1, 2005.

Mesopotamia (*Bet Nahrain*), or the land between the rivers, located in modern-day Iraq, was home to some of the earliest and most advanced civilizations. Mesopotamia encompassed the Sumerian, Akkadian, Babylonian, and Assyrian empires. The Assyrian empire covered the present-day regions of northern Iraq, northwestern Iran, southeastern Turkey and northeastern Syria. The *lingua franca* of Mesopotamia was Aramaic. The language and cultural practices of the Empire continued long after its fall. When Islam began to spread in the 7th century A.D. Assyrians, by now Christians, moved north into mountainous territories to escape subjugation or death and by virtue of their isolation, kept their language and cultural practices alive. Neo-Aramaic, with its many name variations and dialects, is still spoken to this day.

The late 19th and early 20th centuries were eras that brought attention to a once isolated people, when Christian missions from the West discovered their ancient brethren in the Middle East. Assyrians were eager to learn, and delighted in fellowship with the missionaries. They experienced a profound transformation as the missionaries established schools and hospitals, educating them in the Western tradition. The times were rapidly changing. It is in this environment that our story takes place. From the perspective of a young girl, the story is told with great humor and eloquence.

I am grateful for my Assyrian heritage and to my Grandparents for the amazing family they produced. I thank my aunt, Elizabeth Yoel Campbell, for giving me the opportunity to edit her stories, and in so doing, affording me the chance to take a deeper look at my roots. I have often turned to my uncle, William Yoel, to clarify words or geographical locations that were unfamiliar to me; to my aunt, Angela Yoel Vartanian, for moral support, and uncle, Robert Yoseph, for just being part of our family. I regret that my mother, Agnes, and uncle, Homer, did not survive to enjoy their family stories in print. Also, thanks to my father, Malcolm Karam, a great storyteller in his own right, who instilled in me the love of writing. Not least, thanks to my husband Bruce and son Lukas for their moral and technical support, my sister Hilda Karam for her support and knowledge of *leeshanet Suryaye*. Lastly, a big thank you to Jennifer Wood Monroe for her incredible design acumen and patience, and all the friends whose kind words sustained me over the years while **Yesterday's Children** was a never-ending project!

# 1

# Yesterday's Children Growing Up in Persia

Although I am not quite eighty years old, I have yet experienced life as it must have been lived in the middle ages. I was born in 1915, and for the first few years of my life lived in a walled city with great iron studded gates. Inside the fortified city lay narrow cobblestoned streets flanked by two-story high adobe walls that hid private dwellings. Small latticed windows pierced the walls at the highest level and solid, strong doors - always locked - barred entrance to intrusive strangers. What went on behind those doors is impossible to tell. Was it a rich man's abode, light and airy inside with courtyards and fountains; interiors filled with priceless hand-woven carpets, silk cushions, golden ornaments, perfumed lamps, and bejeweled harem wives? Or was it a poor man's home; a warren of dark rooms and darker yet passages, where perhaps twenty families lived four, five, six to a room? No one could tell from the outside. For no one wanted to attract the evil eye of the jealous, or the attention of greedy and fierce tribesmen who, from time to time and without warning, descended on the hapless inhabitants of unwalled cities. They sacked, pillaged and carried off the young women, then withdrew to their mountain fastness where no government troops dared to follow. Who knew if these cutthroat tribal folk would not attempt to come into our guarded city as well?

Our town walls were as thick as they were high. When all the caravans bringing in merchandise from far off places like Samarkand and Bokhara, Isphahan and Khorasan, Baghdad and Basra, and other places to the east were safely in, the gates clanged shut. Afterward, only a special permit from the Governor or knowledge of the secret password could let you in or out.

Inside these thick city walls were granaries and sufficient stores to feed the inhabitants in times of siege or famine. There were also barracks for the soldiers who guarded the walls twenty-four hours a day, men always on the lookout for possible trouble. By sunset the noisy caravans had arrived at their destination to the great *caravansaries*, inns with large courtyards accomodating travelers and puck animals needing food, lodging, and rest for the night after an arduous day-long crossing of the desert, or seemingly interminable mountains. The caravansaries opened out onto the great bazaar creating easy access for traveling merchants to sell their goods, or to barter for the purchase of local wares before making ready for tomorrow's caravan. The great bazaar consisted of acres upon acres of shops laid out on a grid of narrow crisscrossing lanes. Covered and vaulted, the only visible daylight streamed in from skylights set twenty-five feet, or higher, at the apex of domed arches. To us children, the bazaars were an enchantment, a wonder-filled Aladdin's cave; a visit there to be prayed for, or dreamed about.

Just before sunset the streets were swept clean and sprinkled down with water from goatskin bags to cool and settle the parched, dusty ground in preparation for the call to evening prayer. I can still smell the scent of water on baked earth, and the fresh, sweet fragrance of petunias growing in secret gardens behind imposing walls. Then, thin and sweet in the evening air, came the lilting voice of the *muezzin* (he who calls worshippers to prayer) from his high perch in a nearby minaret, that place of honor towering above all other buildings: *"La Allah Alallah, Mohammed Rasul Allah"* (Allah is great and Mohammed is his messenger). Wherever he was at the time, a Muslim spread out his prayer rug and answered the call to prayer. He turned toward Mecca and performed rituals of his faith openly and unselfconciously. With prayers over and the muezzin silent, the devotee picked up his rug, shook and folded it reverently, and went home to his waiting family.

It was a quiet time out on the streets at this hour, the city gates were now locked and barred against the evils of the night. But high up on the rooftops it was bright and alive with laughter and joyful anticipation. At our home, as in every other, the oil lamps were being lit. Some lamps were very beautiful, fashioned from gold and adorned with ruby glass, while those in the homes of poorer families were made of inexpensive tin. With lamps and lanterns illuminated, tablecloths laid, and dishes set out, this was the time for families to gather for their evening meal; the time for fragrant pilaf, spiced lamb kabobs, chilled *sharbat* (a cold fruit drink), yogurt, and fresh fruits from our lands. In warm weather most people had their evening meals and slept on the flat rooftops of their houses, for the city was malarial and troublesome mosquitoes stayed close to the ground in the damp vegetation of low-lying gardens. The roofs were enclosed by high parapets for safety and to guard privacy, but you knew that people all over town were in their rooftop patios. One could hear laughter and whispering voices nearby, and see reflected light from lanterns on parapet walls in all directions, stretching for what seemed like forever.

By the time our evening meal was over the blackness of night was upon us. All around, voices had stilled to the hushed tones of more intimate conversations. In my family, baby Angel and the two middle children, Willie and Agnes, were soon fast asleep in their cots in a private little corner behind a chimney stack. On another stack, outlined against the night sky, our regular summer tenant, Father Stork, stood on one leg guarding his mate and her chicks. The servants had, by now, cleared remnants of our dinner and retired to their own quarters somewhere in the depths of the house. Finally, my older brother, Homer, and I were sent off to sleep under the magical night sky as the deep silence of evening descended, wrapping us in slumberous peace.

Often I would lie awake on my back gazing at the stars so far, far away. On one particularly clear night they seemed closer than usual. I felt that I could stretch out my arm and pick a star, keeping it for my very own. I would gaze and gaze, fighting off sleep, wondering if somewhere out there among those millions of worlds there were other little girls who would like to be my friends, to come down and play with me. The spectacular night sky brought to mind my kinship to those long gone Assyro-Babylonian ancestors who were the first to transform the practice of stargazing into the art of astrology, then into the science of astronomy.

Suddenly, something startled me. Except for the perennial chatter of our river, the Sufi Chai, just outside the city gates, there was usually no audible sound, light, or whisper at this hour. I listened carefully and then…yes, I heard it more clearly. It was the sound of donkey hooves on the cobblestoned street below. I ran to the parapet and climbed onto a chair to get a better look, and in the pitch dark I could see a lantern bobbing up and down in the distance. As the lantern approached, for a brief moment, a man came into my line of vision. He ran ahead, lighting the way for his master who was riding astride a donkey. The master was a *mullah* (an Islamic cleric) on a mission of mercy, perhaps going to the bedside of a dying man. For no one, unless on illicit business, would be out at this time of night without a pass, or knowledge of the official password. Papa, being a doctor, always knew the password, which was changed every few days. The "word" was passed directly to him by his friend, the Governor. Papa was at the Governor's compound almost every day, as there was always someone sick in his large household.

As the mullah's light was swallowed up by the night, I could hear the town crier's voice approaching. Every few yards he stopped and called out at the top of his voice, "It is now ten o'clock (for instance) and all is well. Sleep well all you true believers, for Allah is great." Then he, too, vanished from sight. I still did not want to go back to bed, because I was waiting for something special to happen. Once again, I heard clippity-clop, clippity-clop, this time the sound of horse's hooves on cobblestones, and the chink of metal on metal. When they came into view, by the light of their lanterns I could see that they were fierce looking men armed to the teeth. They would have to be, for this was the night watch, and because of them we all slept more soundly. They, too, vanished into the velvet darkness, the noise of their passage gradually diminishing with distance.

It was silent again, all the world asleep. Father Stork remained seemingly awake, still on one leg, guarding his precious nestlings. In the deep and eerie silence, I imagined I could hear dim, unintelligible fairy

4

voices singing songs of Arabian Nights, enticing me from the stars above. All of a sudden, I was afraid and felt so alone in the world that I no longer liked the night, or the mysteries it held. I scurried to Mama's and Papa's bed and nestled in between them, to be held safely in their arms. Once comforted, the night no longer held fearsome secrets and I drifted off to sleep.

When I awoke, the balmy dawn of a new day was unfolding. The night-time breeze had quieted, and the poplar leaves that had been rustling, as if singing lullabies to slumbering children, were quiet too. All of nature seemed suspended, waiting for sunrise and the regeneration of life.

## Our Family

Our family consists of Papa, Mama, Grandma Ghozal, and five children. Angel is the baby and her name suits her perfectly. She hardly ever cries, amuses herself happily, and is attempting to crawl. The next older child is Agnes. She is adorable with large dark eyes, creamy skin, and curly hair. She once met with an unfortunate accident caused by my energetic brother Homer. He was vigorously wielding a wooden sword which met with Agnes's face, piercing both cheeks. After a painful healing there remained no visible scars, only two enticing dimples and an enchanting smile. Agnes loves playing with her dolls and with Angel, which leaves Willie very lonely in the middle. Homer and I aren't ready to include him in our games as he is too young to keep up with us when we hurtle up and down stairs, or slide down banisters. Willie is a sturdy and cuddly child, always setting progressive goals for himself and achieving them without fuss or fanfare.

I am the next eldest child, and according to the servants, a pampered pest who has her poor Papa, the doctor, wrapped around her little finger. I can certainly wheedle most things out of him if I set my mind to it. I know the power of my enchanting smile and I can whine and cry and keep the tears flowing until the poor man, so soft where his wife and children are concerned, gives in.

Finally, there's Homer, the eldest. He is tall for his age, handsome, and clever. He is also inventive in devising mischief and planning getaways through the interconnecting buildings which encircle our three courtyards. The courtyards have three solid gates and a doorman who admits patients to Papa's medical clinic. He is not permitted to let us leave the grounds unless we are accompanied by an attendant.

Homer is my closest friend and playmate. Outside of the high-walled school compound (especially in winter) we don't see much of our friends, except on special occasions when they come visiting with their parents. My brother is also my Knight in Shining Armor. He assures me that if those thieving Kurds ever come down from their mountain lairs to take me away, he will personally kill them all! At this, he draws out his wooden *khanjal*, the same one that pierced Agnes's cheeks, and with a blood curdling yell whirls the thing around and around his head until I get dizzy.

# 2

## Maragha and Urmia: The Assyrian Presence

Our walled city of Maragha was in the Turkish speaking province of Azerbaijan, northwestern Iran. It was located about 140 miles south of the Russian border, and eighty to ninety miles east of Turkey. Part of Azerbaijan province lay north of the River Aras in what is now Armenia and the country of Azerbaijan. At the time of World War I the population of greater Maragha, combining those living inside the city walls with those living outside, was about forty thousand people.

The River Aras, which was the boundary line between Russia and Persia, was not very wide. You could practically hopscotch across it. My friend Giohar's father was chief of customs in Julfa at the time, and oftentimes when I stayed with her we watched the changing of the guard on our side of the river. The bridge and river were two thirds Persian and one third Russian. The guard from our side marched on the double to meet his Russian counterpart at the barred gates across the bridge, guns at the ready, swords hanging in scabbards at his hip. They met, saluted smartly, and then marched back, each keeping a measured pace in order to reach the opposite banks at the same time.

The township of Julfa was low lying and very hot in summer; it had the largest black scorpions I have seen anywhere. They were, perhaps, four to five inches long possessing a fatal sting.

Ties between the divided sister states were well established, both being Muslim and Turkish speaking. About ninety-five percent of the population of Azerbaijan Province was Shiite, and the rest Sunni Muslims, Christians, and other minorities. The number of Christians dwindled to less than one percent over the years. Because of the strong ties between the sister states, and the proximity of the Russian border, most people spoke at least a modicum of Russian. The Persian government discouraged the spread of the Russian language, or friendly relations with the Russians. Over the centuries there had been many wars fought between the two countries, but despite great odds, Persia managed to keep most of its territorial integrity. That it was a buffer state between the two great powers, Great Britain and Russia, was helpful.

Maragha was founded by Assyrian Christians in the early years of the faith. The Mar in Maragha means "saint" in the Assyrian language, and the name Acha gradually corrupted into agha meaning "sir" in Farsi, the Persian language. Assyrian Nestorians are said to have settled there as early as the 11th century A.D. Nestorianism, which got its name from Bishop Nestorius, Patriarch of Constantinople (428-32 A.D.), was made the official Christian religion of the realm by Firouz the Second in the year 480 A.D. He protected the Christians by law from Zoroastrian persecution. After the Arab conquest of Persia and the subsequent spread of Islam in the early eighth century, the government granted religious freedom to its Christian subjects and passed a law of official protection for all its minorities. Although the law offered protected status to our Mesopotamian ancestors, developers of the most flourishing civilization in the Middle East, as a vanquished people they were required to make tribute for their protection. The law of protection still stood, though it had often been violated over the years at times when the government was too weak to enforce it against random discriminatory aggression.

Aside from its bazaars and surrounding walls, Maragha had little left of the architectural gems built by the great Mongol conquerers. Much had been lost by way of wars, fires, and the ravages of time. Judging from the physical features of some citizens, however, the Mongols may have left something more permanent, DNA!

Three or four miles outside the city there was a great labyrinthine cave system. Because the caves were extensive and dangerous, explorers used balls of string to mark their pathway into the caves and track their way out again. The caves were a great treasury of fossils and ancient animal bones. In the early part of the twentieth century there were several

American expeditions sent by various universities to explore them. My parents were hosts to some members of these expeditions and I can remember the men washing, sorting, and meticulously numbering the bones. They made sketches of how an animal might look when the bones were assembled. Grotesque and fantastic shapes emerged of animals that had been extinct for centuries. The caves were never fully explored and their remote recesses may still hold treasures that silently guard the drama of ages past.

Nearby there were mineral springs, noisy and effervescent. Our parents would take us to the springs several times a year well prepared with jars, lemons, and sugar so we could make ourselves exquisite lemonade, drinking until we could hold no more. Over the centuries the mineral waters had created fantastic shapes with some very life-like figures around the base of the hill. One configuration reminded me of our bakehouse with the in-ground oven and the bakers busy at their jobs, ready to slam the bread dough onto the sides of the oven.

Maragha was about fifteen miles east of Persia's only large inland lake, Lake Urmia, a salt lake. It lay at the center of a lush fruit and wheat growing district. Many varieties of grapes were grown here, in addition to the most delicious pears, apples, peaches, apricots, and assorted varieties of cherries and nuts. Maragha had few rivals to the quality of its abundant fruit, with the exception of its sister city, Urmia, situated on the western shores of the lake. There was just one way in which Maragha definitely surpassed Urmie, however, and that was with our grape molasses called *nepookhta*. Made from a special type of grape nepookhta is thick like yoghurt, amber in color and smooth to the tongue. We ate the grainy looking molasses on bread with clotted cream for breakfast - truly the nectar and ambrosia of the gods. Whenever I asked what made our nepookhta so much nicer than any other, I was told it was because of our special soil. For many years I used to wonder how anything so delicious could be made of common garden dirt!

There were also orchards of huge mulberry trees bearing thousands of luscious, purplish black berries. Homer, Willie, and I kept hundreds of pet silkworms that fed only on mulberry leaves. Twice a week we would clean the drawer slots of their little habitat, and visit the nearby mulberry grove to refresh their food supply. It was fascinating to watch the little caterpillars eat and spin their silk cocoons in preparation for their metamorphoses over the winter, emerging as exotic moths in the spring.

In nearby Urmia, or Urmie as we Assyrians called it, there was an Assyrian population of about five to six thousand people. They all seemed to have the greenest of thumbs and made the land around them blossom prolifically. We had a number of relatives who had settled in Urmie, some on Mama's side of the family and others from Papa's, after managing to flee the deathly massacres of Armenians and Assyrians in Turkey.

Lake Urmia had several mountain streams flowing into it, but since there was no outlet the water grew to be very salty and heavy. The lake was slowly shrinking from excessive evaporation. Approaching by car over the gently sloping terrain, Lake Urmia looked like a deep blue gem surrounded by a glittering diadem. You could see the salt deposits surrounding it from miles away, shining and shimmering, blinding the eyes from the pale blue edges to its deep blue, sapphire heart. Because the lake water was so heavily saturated with salt, it was not possible to dive into it, nor could you drown. There was no jetty to get to the deeper water so we had to wade through an endless stretch of malodorous, clinging, sucking, needle sharp, salt encrusted mud, only to come out with our eyes stinging and bodies itching. It took Herculean effort to wade through the mud to reach the fresh water stream flowing into the lake. By the time we got there our hair had dried and stood up like pointed white stalagmites. Like Lot's wife of Biblical fame we had turned into salt encrusted, living, itching, suffering statues swearing never to go near the lake again. But we did, of course, because it was fun and the mud was said to have curative properties.

The lake was about twenty-five miles across at its widest point and about one hundred miles long. Twice daily steamers left from different ports carrying passengers and goods, crisscrossing paths near the middle. One crossing was particularly memorable for me. The sounds of animated singing from the passing boat still rings in my ears.

Homer and Willie were going on a two-week excursion to Kara Dagh (Black Rock) with their scout group, so Mama thought it would be fun for the rest of us to have a holiday together in Urmie, to visit relatives we had not seen for a while.

There was great excitement and anticipation. The seamstress and her apprentice came every day to make holiday clothing for us girls, shirts and shorts for the boys and a couple of dresses for Mama. Clothes could not be bought ready-made back then. Everyhing was custom-made by a seamstress for the women and girls, and men's and boy's suits were tailor-made in the bazaar. Our seamstress worked out of her home, but came to us regularly three or four days a month, or more often if we needed her.

We left Tabriz on the same day that Homer and Willie were delivered into the safekeeping of their scoutmaster. We boarded the train to Sufian and changed to the single line west connecting with the steamer service at the northeastern end of the lake. Another steamer, gleaming white on the deep blue water, was passing us from about three hundred yards away, carrying a group of young Americans (Presbyterian missionaries and some college students) to Tabriz. Everyone waved enthusiastically to each other. As they approached we could hear them singing at the top of their voices, "My bonnie lies over the ocean, my bonnie lies over the sea." We joined in too, Angel's sweet voice, a pure soprano, rising high and clear, and Agnes harmonizing in contralto as naturally as if she has been rehearsing for the part. Gradually, the strains of song died away into the distance. It was quiet again, the water calm and unruffled, and the magical moment in which our lives so briefly touched those of others on the wings of song was already in the past. For a moment I stood there gripping the rail feeling empty. For the first time in my life I was aware that life is transient, that I am mortal and that there is nothing I, or anyone, can do to stop the passage of time.

Once in Urmie, we went in search of a man we had heard about from friends. He and his horse had been a team in a Russian circus and now he operated a horse and buggy service driving tourists who wanted to do "the grand tour" of Urmie and the surrounding villages. Mama had her

11

heart set on a well-sprung carriage with comfortably upholstered seats and shady hood, but soon we brought her around to our way of thinking. "A singing coachman and a darting horse, Mama! Please, Mama, please. We'll never see the likes of it again!"

The coachman, Mr. Yuav, was everything we had hoped for. His cart was piled high with clean, fluffy cushions fragrant with lavender. For the next week he became our personal chauffeur, arriving every morning at nine o'clock sharp, ready to take us to the village of our choice. We had great fun driving around in the cart with Mr.Yuav. He had an impressive tenor voice and while we joined in, he made the horse go through paces learned from his circus days, prancing to the rhythm of our singing. He entertained us with stories about the founding of Urmie, of wars, massacres, personal courage and sacrifice, and the survival of a small Christian ethnic group, ours, living there for centuries while surrounded by a tightly closing ring of Muslims.

Local Assyrian legend claimed that Urmia was founded by one of Assyria's ancient kings, King Sargon the Second, in 720 B.C. He named the city Ur-mia, City of Water. After the Second World War, Reza Shah Pahlavi visited Urmia on his "triumphal tour" and changed its name to Rezaieh, City of Reza, in his own honor. Ironically, he never visited there again. As an Assyrian, I still refer to the city as Urmie, or Ur-mia, City of Water, city of Sargon.

There are few Assyrians left in Urmie now. After about 1,500 years of occupancy they grew tired of being isolated in the midst of Islam. After the fall of Christian Russia to communism, the weary Assyrians started looking westward for a new place to call home, where they could settle free of anxiety. The American Presbyterian mission had significantly influenced the lifestyle and culture of Assyrians since the latter part of the nineteenth century. They had provided schools and hospitals, effectively paving their way westward. Today there are more Assyrians in the U.S. than in Mesopotamia.

The Assyrian villages we explored were all very clean and tidy, humble houses constructed of hand-made mud bricks looking neat and in good repair. The surrounding local orchards produced fruit matching the quality of our Maragha grown fruit. I loved seeing the villagers and feeling our ethnic connection that we have had in common since ancient times.

On the outskirts of the village Spourghan, there were an extensive series of high mounds and hillocks composed of ashes, which had been trampled solid through the passage of time. They were relics of Zoroastrian worship, evidence of the perpetual sacred fires, of temples, and the hearth. Zoroastrians too, had long gone from Urmia. Their worship was now centered in and around the city of Yazd, in central Persia, an attractive city home to numerous ancient buildings. The Zoroastrian religion mandates cleanliness of person, word, deed, and surroundings. It is forbidden to defile the earth or desecrate the sacred fire. For this reason, they neither burn nor bury their dead, but expose them to vultures and other birds of prey on soaring fortress-like towers called Towers of Silence. Before the Arabians swept through the Middle East swiftly spreading Islam, the Persian people had practiced Zoroastrianism. There was a rumor that Mohammad Reza Shah was Zoroastrian, but converted to Islam upon ascending the Peacock Throne.

After an hour of sightseeing amid the mountains of ash we picnicked in a nearby mulberry grove. I laid back lazily and descended into a daydream about mulberry trees and ashes, ashes and Zoroastrians, Zoroastrian women and mulberries, and Yazd. In this dreamy state I remembered an amusing story that is told about the women of Yazd.

It is said that the young women of Yazd are stricken each summer by a mysterious disease which leaves them entirely sapped of will, or willingness, to carry on. They approach their husbands, addressing them in the flowery language of their region, saying: "Oh, my husband, beloved father of my children! The summer sickness is upon me once again. I know that I cannot go on serving you the way you deserve until I've eaten my fill of luscious mulberries such as those an elderly friend of my family grows in his country garden. They are so unlike the dried up bird droppings that go for mulberries growing on our city trees! I am sure that this old man will gladly put me up at his place during the mulberry season. Then I shall return to you recovered from my illness and once more become the willing and able wife I used to be!"

The husband, for once, does not ask awkward questions, nor object in any way. Perhaps he also has an "elderly" country cousin sickening for city grown mulberries. The wife, already packed, is soon astride her donkey and on her way. That is why, on a certain day in early summer when mulberries are in season, a traveler approaching Yazd may see an unusually large number of unattended women heading away from the city, disappearing into country lanes that lead to shady mulberry groves. The men waiting for them are not old and wizened as the wives have described them, but young, vital, and eager.

In due course, mulberry season is over, and the wives journey homeward looking radiant and rejuvenated, as if they have discovered Eldorado and have dipped into the Fountain of Youth! The husbands, too, receiving them with open arms, look happy, well-fed and well-looked after. They carry on with life together, after the brief interval, as if they had just been married. Edward Stack of the Bengal Civil Service makes reference to this custom in his book *Six Months in Persia*, dated 1881.

After our memorable holiday, we returned to Tabriz the day before Homer and Willie were due to return from their Kara Dagh excursion. We went to watch the scouts marching through the streets, banners fluttering in the breeze, drums beating rhythm in time with the flutes, and the boys marching proudly to report to the Head Scout before officially disbanding. Willie came first with the youngest group. We cheered him, waving madly. Then came Homer's troupe. When Homer saw Mama he raised a large earthenware pot over his head and yelled, "Mama, Mama, I've brought you some honey all the way from Kara Dagh." Mama was so proud that she boasted to everyone about it.

Finally, the boys arrived home and the earthenware pot was opened with great ceremony. Inside there was a large, glazed wooden spoon and about two tablespoons of honey left sticking to the sides. Ever the generous person, Homer had not been able to refuse his friends a taste.

The pot and spoon had made repeated rounds on the journey home bringing sweetness and comfort to weary, hungry, homesick boys.

# 3

# Sufi Chai and No-Ruz: The Sufi River and Persian New Year

The snow had been particularly heavy one winter and the mountain passes surrounding us on all sides were impassable for days. With the spring equinox and the Persian *No-Ruz*, New Year (though, literally meaning "new day"), just round the corner on the twenty-first of March, there was still no sign of a thaw, or spring. We feared that No-Ruz would be lost to us forever, just as spring seemed to be. Even the storks had deserted us. Every morning we looked hopefully at the sky, but it remained leaden. On the roof, high above our heads, the chimney stack stood stark against the sky with last year's battered nest empty and desolate, waiting to be repaired and reoccupied. We children vied with each other as to who among us would be the harbinger of the good news that the storks had finally arrived.

The ground was iron hard so it was a good time for skating. Any flat, open space we could find we flooded with water and let winter make slippery skating rinks to the detriment, and loss of dignity, of our solid elder citizens. A heavy snowfall one night blanketed everything with a thick coating of white. Baby Snowman turned into a mound and Mr. and Mrs. Snowman acquired funny shapes through their sudden and excessive gain in weight.

Soon after lunch one day, in the brief afternoon sunshine, wrapped up to the ears we were loaded onto our two sleds, I holding Angel and Homer holding Agnes with Willie at the back. We were pulled through the courtyard gates, over three hundred yards of snowbound street and through the enormous city gates to the wide river bank, now transformed by snow into a fairyland stretching away and out of sight. There were no evergreen trees there so all the bare branches were covered with thick, pristine snow, shining with myriad jeweled points in the weak frosty sunshine of the winter's afternoon.

The Sufi Chai River has its headwaters in the peaks of the Sahand Mountains just north of Maragha. These are the tallest mountains in our province of Azerbaijan, the highest point being over 12,000 feet. When the spring thaw begins it is as though a wild beast is unleashed. For now, though, Sufi Chai is sullen and has not changed its tune for many days; it just croons a gentle lament of whoosh, whoosh, whoosh. When it does change its tune we will know that the thaw has begun and that spring and No-Ruz will soon be here. Our Sufi Chai can sing and it can speak. It expresses itself in many moods; now a small noisy ripple, now bored and edgy tinged with a deep growl as it sweeps across small rocks and pebbles, grinding them against each other into sand, now frenzied and frisky, and finally, with a deafening roar its tall, forward leaping waves flecked with foam, tempestuous and angry. For now though, Sufi Chai is practically comatose, the larger boulders sitting high and dry and indifferent to the river's mood.

A thunderous crash wakes up everyone in the night. The river has finally come to life, its mighty roar making the ground tremble with the first onslaught of springtime's raging floodwaters. First one, then the other of the little ones starts to cry. Mama and Papa are up, lamps are lit, fires raked and stoked and the pandemonium quieted. Reassured at last, we finally settle contentedly in our beds, and return to dreamland.

When we wake it is to beautiful, warm sunshine. The snow melts rapidly turning into muddy slush underfoot. A group of snow-shovelers has arrived with large, square shovels and is sweeping and shoveling the snow into mounds to cart away. Inside the house, a major spring cleaning is underway to prepare for the friends who will come calling at No-Ruz. There is a delicious aroma of cooking and spices in the air. Cupboards groan with enough goodies to feed a small army. A few traditional sweets, such as Turkish delight, saffron, or sweet rice cookies are purchased, but most of the food has been grown, raised, ground, churned, dried, and preserved at home from the produce of our own fields and orchards located across the Sufi Chai River.

Mama has a special open house for her Muslim friends for, being veiled, they are not allowed to mix socially with men other than their own husbands and family. The Muslim ladies call on us separately in twos and threes, arriving in closed carriages accompanied by an older woman attendant, a driver and groom and, when necessary, an armed side-rider. It is always exciting for us girls when the Muslim ladies visit. I like the colorful clothes they wear under the chador and I love the chador, too. I would like to have a chador of my own and have pestered Mama many times about it, but she always says, "No, no, no." Surprisingly, even Papa is adamant on that score. When aprons go missing from the kitchen they are found pinned to my hair then tied around my middle like a chador, with my face covered and only an eye showing.

The chador is a semicircular piece of cloth made from black, heavy silk or fine wool and is long enough to cover its wearer from the bridge of her nose to over her head and then flow freely almost to the ground at her back. A beautifully embroidered back panel joins the two ends from the waist down, which is then tied underneath the veil at the back, like an apron. Because women are only able to show their eyes to the world they make the best of it and have developed eye make-up into an art. They look beautiful and speak dramatically with their eyes. Many a man has been enchanted and fallen in love at the sight of those mysterious, dark eyes.

When women go out they actually wear three layers of clothing. Under the chador they wear black pantaloons and stockings and black shoes. The younger ones sometimes wear kid shoes with upturned toes, the tops gaily embroidered with geometric designs, and crowned with a cheeky pompom. Underneath all the black covering is the colorful, traditional clothing that is so charming to me compared to our more modern Western dress.

Papa's Muslim friends and patients always come loaded with gifts for everyone in our family; small hand-woven carpets, curly black lambs, a pony or a colt, amber and turquoise beads for us girls. They are very generous, considering that they own rich lands, farms, and even whole villages. We have many visitors at No-Ruz, some unknown to us children, and all bearing gifts. On this particular year, the Governor gives Papa a beautiful white Arabian horse named Sultan. The horse comes with its own Newfoundland dog, or is it a huge dog with its own horse? Those two belong together, and to each other. They have grown up together as colt and puppy, chasing each other across meadows, neighing and barking, answering each other's call, and at night nestling together in the same stall. In time, they accepted Papa as their own, making the twosome a threesome. People everywhere stop and watch them go by. In Islam dogs are considered unclean, and are never allowed inside the house as families do not make pets of them. Our Muslim friends are always amazed at the way we pamper our dogs.

The poor, who are not required to pay Papa's medical fees or for medicine, come without gifts and go home laden. They receive the seven traditional sweets called *yeddi lokhum*, nuts and dried fruits of the land, gifts for their families, and some money placed in small calico bags that Grandma has been sewing for days. There is no paper money in use as people have not taken kindly to it, so all transactions are carried out in coins of copper, silver, or gold. There is no shame attached to the fact that less fortunate citizens come to the well-to-do expecting, and receiving, gifts. They come prepared with large sacks that they fill and carry home on their backs. This is the custom of the land. Bounty flows in wondrous plenty from the top to the lowest level, a system that has worked well for centuries. Additionally, the well-to-do employ a community of servants and staff that they retain for life. These are workers in the field, the bake house, shepherds, grooms, cart and carriage drivers, groundskeepers, nannies, cooks, and many others. All these people have job security living under the protection of the great family they serve for their entire lives.

At No-Ruz the streets are frenzied with activity and teeming with wall-to-wall people. The street vendors, competing with each other for business, call out their merchandise of silk ribbons, ornate jewelery, transparent veils and scarves, laces, tassels and pompoms, perfumes, and *kohl* (eye shadow). Everything is colorful and bejeweled, the veils and scarves silver and gold threaded. In fact, each vendor sells goods much-loved by harem wives and frivolous little girls like me. What fun it is to watch him open all the little drawers and compartments of the carrying case slung across his shoulders and opened in front to display his enchanting, shiny wares.

During this holiday season we see a diversity of races, religions, tribes, and classes, each recognizable by their speech and tribal costumes. Now comes a small group of Kurds down from their mountain homes and all eyes are on them as they pass. They are well aware of being watched and are playing up to the crowd by walking tall, rolling their eyes, and twirling their already well-pointed moustaches. A common peculiarity of their race is eyes of two colors, one brown the other blue or green, or one blue and the other green. The men wear turbans, yards of material twisted and rolled around a form and worn like a hat with a jeweled clasp or ornament in front. Their pantaloons are long and baggy and they wear beautifully hand embroidered vests over their floppy sleeved shirts. Their pants are held up with yards of rolled material wound around their waists, in the same manner as the turban, with a gun and khanjal tucked into the folds. A bandolier of shells, or bullets, is worn across the chest. They also carry a rifle slung across their backs. When unaffected by trachoma, a common viral eye disease, they look very handsome, romantic and fearsome. No one fears them now, hoewever, because they have entered the city by means of a bond, having left important hostages at the citadel in exchange for gaining entry. Here in the east, exchange of hostages is a common way of life and works well in difficult situations.

The scribe is in his usual corner sitting cross-legged on a carpet square behind a small, low desk doing a roaring business writing letters, bills, or petitions. The letters are very flowery, filled with compliments. To

ﾠﾠﾠ

straightforward sentences like "How are you?" and "We are all well," are added embellishments such as "Respected Sir and beloved Son, the day of your birth was, and remains, blessed," or, "The mercy of Allah saw us through the ills and chills of winter and Allah's blessings have always been on our house since that day," and so on. Persian script reads from right to left, as does Arabic, and the language of my own people, Syriac, which is one of the most ancient alphabets in the world. Ancient Greeks developed their own alphabet from the example of the Assyrian alphabet, and the names of the letters in the two languages remain similar to this day.

There are other fascinating sights and sounds, so many that we cannot take them all in; the story teller, *ipa chekhan* (tightrope walker), the singers and dancers. One day soon, we may get to visit the Story Teller in his corner and be mesmerized by his beautiful voice as he weaves and spins his tales. Each word is music to our ears, flowing smoothly like the amber beads he thumbs continuously as he speaks.

## 4

# To Kurdistan: Iodine "The Miracle Cure"

Clippity-clop, clippity-clop, clippity-clop, the sound of horse's hooves on cobble stones, approaching quickly. In the eerie silence of the night the sound carries like gunshot, menacing and mysterious. I turn over to go back to sleep, but someone shakes me awake.

"Bess, Bess, are you awake? Wake up, Bess."

"Go away, leave me alone," I mumble.

"Come on Bess, wake up, it is the Kurds, a lot of them, they've come for Papa."

At the word "Kurd" I suddenly become wide awake and sit bolt upright. "Kurds, where?"

"There in the courtyard." Homer drags me to the window. We see three of them down below, illuminated by lanterns, armed to the teeth and pacing impatiently, waiting. In the outer courtyard there are more lanterns and other voices, and in the street we hear the restless shuffle of horses, the clank of metal on metal.

"Who are they? Do you recognize anyone in that lot?"

"Yes, that one," he points. "He is one of Mohammed Agha's men, the one who gave me the wooden khanjal. There must have been more fighting among the tribes."

Mama and Papa come to us, and we run to Papa's embrace. Willie joins us too, rubbing his eyes, walking drunkenly, still half asleep. Papa always comes to say goodbye when he is called away. Mama has been crying and we start crying too, though we do not quite know why. She hates it when Papa has to go into Kurdistan. Throughout the ages Kurds have been one of the greatest scourges of Eastern Christians. When the Christian minorities were not strong enough to protect themselves, Kurds

22

took advantage by looting and killing people in their villages. But Papa is a doctor, a surgeon, a healer, and as such is much respected. Among the tribes, when on a mission of mercy, he is virtually untouchable. A Kurdish agha's word is his bond, and he'd rather shoot his own son (even if only in the foot!) than lose face by breaking his word.

Out on the street the Night Watch is getting impatient. They are anxious to see the menacing, always touchy, and fractious Kurds out of town with the gates safely barred behind them. One of the Kurds has Papa's saddle bags, the other his medicine chest and surgical kit, tools for any contingency a lone doctor can attend to. Sultan is also edgy, neighing impatiently for his master, as is Khan, the dog. But they will not be going along as Papa hates exposing them to the dangers of a hazardous journey such as this, or taking them into the middle of a tribal war.

We hear the street door being barred and bolted, a command, a shuffling into position, whispered talk, a clanging of metal, and the sound of horses' hooves, diminishing with distance. Mama, eyes still red from weeping, kisses me and tucks me in, then takes the boys to their own beds in the adjoining room. My two darling little sisters, tucked snugly in their cots, have slept soundly through all the excitement.

"Good night, Mama."

"Good night, my child, sleep tight."

Lights are out. A deep silence descends on us, wrapping us in its suffocating folds. I am only too glad to cover my head with my quilt and go back to sleep. I wake briefly, as the faintest streak of dawn shows through a chink in the curtains. A solitary cock crows in the distance, a lonely, mournful sound in the eerie silence of pre-dawn.

A moment later, or so it seems to me, I wake up to brilliant sunshine and an exciting new day. At breakfast we are amused to learn that Willie does not remember any of last night's events. He thinks we are pulling his leg, as we often do, and nothing we say will convince him otherwise. Even Mama, who has been looking sad, starts to laugh. Willie is such a clown. Mama can never be angry with him for long as he immediately puts on a doleful face and says and does comical things until she starts to laugh, forgetting her anger.

After breakfast of *pirrini* (porridge), eggs or cheese, bread and butter with nepookhta or honey, and a selection of fresh or dried fruits, Mama doles out our daily dose of *quina-quina*, for this city is malarial and the mosquitoes are very bad right now. Quina-quina is quinine, the name Native Americans gave the shrub from which they extracted the powder to keep malaria at bay, and that in revenge for all that the white man did to them, they kept a secret for many years.

"Children, Mr. Gregorian will soon be here to take you out, so keep yourselves clean, please." Then to Pari Baji who looks after us: "Pari Baji, don't let them get into mischief, please, and they are not to go outside until Mr. Gregorian arrives."

Mama leaves us, and after a few minutes of hedging and fidgeting, Pari Baji leaves us too, telling us to be good, and that she will be back shortly. But we know from past experience that she'll be gone for quite some time, and decide to play for a while at something safe and clean; something like Doctor, Nurse, and Patient.

Pari Baji and the gatekeeper share a great (and it seems important) secret, so whenever she gets an opportunity she goes to see him and they whisper together. Homer, ever curious, has on several occasions sneaked in close enough to learn the nature of this secret, but to no avail. He thinks that the secret must be really important as they take care that no one is nearby and whisper so softly that not even Homer, who has such sharp ears, can hear a word. If only we could discover their secret. But more importantly, we must get on with our game of Doctor, Nurse and Patient. Now that Willie is able to keep up with Homer and me, he joins us in our games. Pari Baji will not be back anytime soon, so we settle down to our "nice, quiet" game without fear of harassment or interference.

We already have a clinic set up in the small storage room off the living room. We have a small table and chairs, various toys, a collection of assorted bandage ends, gauze, long toothpick-type swabs, and a small packet of clinically sealed squares of white paper. A single dose of powdered medicine is carefully weighed, or measured, and dispensed straight onto a paper square, then folded in a special way to prevent spillage. The medicine is then administered from paper to tongue, as we know only too well. We also have a small scale, scissors, assorted bottles, and some old medical journals to which we "refer" from time to time, outdoing each other with our "ohs and ahas." All we need now is some medicine. As Papa's clinic is strictly taboo to us, our only other source of pharmaceuticals is the kitchen. Homer goes to see what he can find without attracting too much attention. Soon he returns with a cloth sack of flour, a pot of nepookhta, and an earthenware pitcher of water. Now we are all set.

Big brother says that, as a doctor is more important than a nurse, his title should be spelled in all capital letters as "DOCTOR." Nurse, who is next in importance, should be spelled as "Nurse." While the patient, being the least important, should be spelled in all lower case letters as "patient." Willie, as the patient, objects, but because he cannot read or write yet, he will never know the difference. I want to object too, but change my mind. After all, as a doctor, Papa is the most important person we know. To us he is more important than the Governor, more important than the *aghas* and *khans* (rulers) of Mian-do-ab and Sayin-kala, and the khans of the mountain tribes. He is so important they always send an escort of a dozen or so men to take him to the tribes and bring him back safely. For a while we toy with the idea that Papa may even be more important than the Shah himself, but decide not to press that point, for the Shah has declared himself *Shah-han-Shah*, King of Kings. Everyone kneels down to him, for he is Lord of all Persia.

We press on with our pharmaceutical work weighing and wrapping the "medicinal" flour as we have seen it done by Papa many times before. Unfortunately, with three pairs of pushing and shoving hands most of the flour ends up on our clothes and on the floor. But no matter, we have enough potions wrapped and ready for immediate use. The potion packets being prepared and out of the way, we mix the nepookhta with water to formulate a "cough syrup." Nepookhta, unlike sugar cane molasses, is delicious, so delicious in fact, that three pairs of hands dip and mix and lick all at the same time. We finally manage to get some of the mixture into the bottles, thinking this must surely be the most difficult job in the world. At last, the job is done and there must be three or four teaspoons of cough syrup in each bottle. Now the drama unfolds as we play...

## Iodine - The Miracle Cure

DOCTOR: Clean the table please, Nurse. We must prepare for our first patient.

Nurse: Yes, DOCTOR.

(She wipes the table with one of Mama's best white damask dinner napkins.)

DOCTOR: Where is the iodine, Nurse?

Nurse: Iodine? We don't have any.

DOCTOR: What, no iodine? You can't cure a patient without iodine. Oh, never mind, I know where I can lay  my hands on a bottle. (DOCTOR leaves quietly.)

Nurse: (Horrified, she calls out) Not from Papa's clinic?

DOCTOR: No, no, don't worry – it's from the medicine chest upstairs. I think there is a bottle of it up there. You can't cure a patient without iodine. (DOCTOR returns in a few moments with an almost full bottle of iodine. Nurse notices that he looks terrible. His clothes, face and the hair showing from under his cap are all sticky with nepookhta and he is sprinkled with flour all over. Nurse looks down at her own clothes and starts to have doubts about the game they are playing, but only for a brief moment.)

DOCTOR: Show our first patient in please, Nurse.

Nurse: You may come in now, patient (patient comes in groaning.)

DOCTOR: Now then, Mr.Willie, what seems to be the matter?

Nurse: He is sick, can't you see?

DOCTOR: Quiet, Nurse, let the patient speak for himself.

patient: I have a sore throat, sore tummy, and a broken leg.

DOCTOR: Hmmm . . . are you sure you have just one broken leg?

Nurse: Two broken legs, I think.

DOCTOR: Quiet, Nurse, let the patient speak for himself! Hmm … Yes you're right, Nurse. Two broken legs it    is. But first let us attend to the throat and tummy. Open wide Mr.Willie and say "ahhh."

DOCTOR: It looks bad, very bad. Your tonsils are up and coated with white goo! Iodine swabs please, Nurse, and be quick about it.

Nurse: Yes, DOCTOR, at once.

(DOCTOR and Nurse each try to get to the iodine first. Mr.Willie clamps his mouth tightly shut at the sight of two long iodine saturated swabs trying to get to his throat at the same time. He has had experience with such swabs before. In the scuffle the iodine bottle overturns then over goes the flour, and the nepookhta. Now iodine, nepookhta, and flour are all over everything, everywhere.)

DOCTOR: (Looking horrified) Clean up this mess, Nurse.

(Nurse gives the DOCTOR a dirty look but is cowed by his frown and starts dabbing away with another of Mama's snowy damask napkins. The more she dabs the more it spreads, and the worse it looks.)

DOCTOR: Well, never mind, Nurse, Pari Baji will clean it. She can clean anything.

Nurse: (Pointing at the DOCTOR) Ha, ha, ha, you have an iodine moustache and a floury nepookhta scab on your chin, ha, ha, ha.

DOCTOR: (Wiping with his sleeve) Never mind that, Nurse. Let us attend to this poor patient first.

(Unable to get to the inside of his mouth, DOCTOR and Nurse decide to paint the patient's throat on the outside and then administer his medicine from paper to tongue. Patient starts to cough and splutter, DOCTOR and Nurse each try to pour some nepookhta mixture into his mouth to wash the flour down his throat. The patient now really looks sick, his throat and face covered with iodine stains, his mouth and tongue coated with a gooey looking mess.)

DOCTOR: (Looking smug and self satisfied) That is very good. You will soon feel much better, Mr Willie. Bandages please, Nurse, and the iodine.

Nurse: There is not much iodine left, DOCTOR. I'll bandage one leg and you do the other.

(The patient's legs are soon painted and bandaged.)

DOCTOR: Good, very good. You have done an excellent job, Nurse. Now quick, let us attend to the broken arm and then clean up. Mr. Gregorian will be here soon.

(The patient's arm is soon painted with the miracle tincture and put into a damask napkin sling. The patient, now looking very self-satisfied and pleased with DOCTOR, Nurse, himself, and life in general, hobbles over to a hall stand for one of Papa's walking sticks. DOCTOR and Nurse, looking very unhappy, dab away at sticky hands and faces, floor, and table.)

Nurse: (Brightening) DOCTOR, there is still some iodine left. I am thinking how nice it would be if I could paint the soles of my feet, my palms, and my toe and finger nails with iodine, just like I have seen Muslim ladies henna theirs.

DOCTOR: I don't think that is such a good idea, Bess. Oh all right, but hurry up. I wish Pari Baji would get back before Mama comes down.

(Nurse, not paying attention, peels off her long home-knitted stockings and starts painting. Suddenly Mama's voice brings them all down to earth with a jolt.)

Mama: Children, where are you? I think I hear Mr. Gregorian outside. Pari Baji, get the children's coats quickly, we don't want to keep the man waiting.

(DOCTOR, now reduced to doctor, and Nurse to nurse give each other one horrified look and move to the wall, guarding their backs, or rather, their backsides. Willie, as usual, holds his ground for he has his own way of dealing with such situations.)

Pari Baji has quietly sneaked in, puffing and looking disheveled after trying to beat Mr. Gregorian to the house. She gives us one look and her hands fly to her head gear.

"Pari Baji, Pari Baji, where is that no good woman, where is everybody?" Mama comes in, looks around the room and her hands fly to her head. "You naughty, naughty children, just you wait until I get my hands on you. And you, you Pari Baji, this is the end, you'll have to go, I can no longer put up with your sloppy ways."

Pari Baji looks crestfallen, but not overly concerned. She knows that no matter what happens she will always be well looked after. Doctor and nurse, however, cringe against the wall as Mama starts advancing toward them. Willie begins to clown around. We are suddenly saved! Mr. Gregorian is being shown in. He, too, is speechless for a moment, then he catches sight of Willie. "Ooillie, you poor boy, how did you manage to break three limbs all at the same time?"

There is a moment of utter silence until Mama, losing self-restraint, starts to laugh. Homer and I begin to laugh in sheer relief. Pari Baji hides a giggle behind a demure hand and, finally, Mr. Gregorian joins in the hilarity. I laugh until my sides ache, the relief is so tremendous. Homer and I are laughing, not only because we see the funny side of it all, but also because of the way Mr.Gregorian pronounces Willie's name. In his language, Armenian, there is no "W" sound. As he speaks some English, he tries to pronounce it correctly and overcompensates, so it sounds more like Oo-illie than anything else.

We three are carted off to the bathhouse. Mr. Gregorian promises to come back for us after lunch with the expressed hope that he will find us nice and clean, and ready to go.

# 5

## A Visit to the Bazaar

Finally, the time has come for our visit to the bazaar. Mr. Gregorian comes for us in his newly washed hay cart, which has a carpet on the floor and cushions for us to sit on. The three of us have been washed and scrubbed until our skins are red and tingly. The iodine stains have proven too stubborn to clean so we have acquired a kind of faded, jaundiced look with hangdog expressions on our faces from constant comments on our looks, and the pointing fingers and titters from the young maids.

The little ones have come to see us off. Agnes is crying, because she wants to go with us, and Angel is stretching her little arms to me and Homer pleading to be picked up. But Mama says no, they can't go as they are much too young to handle the jostling and chaos of the bazaars. They stop crying when we promise to bring them each a toy and ribbons for their hair, though Angel prefers eating her ribbons to wearing them.

At the sight of us Mr. Gregorian looks amused and asks if we are the same Homer, Bess, and "Ooilli" who are supposed to go to the bazaar with him. Afraid that we may lose our chance for the outing we assure him that we are the same and ask Mama to confirm it. Everyone looks amused. Mr. Gregorian congratulates Willie on the miraculous recovery he has made from his injuries of that morning. At that comment everyone starts laughing again, with the three of us joining in heartily, though not quite knowing what is so funny. I notice that even Agnes and Angel are delighted. It dawns on me that laughter is a contagious thing, and I can see why Mama cannot be angry with Willie for very long.

When we arrive at the bazaar we stop for a moment at the main entrance. There are actually several entrances giving access to different sections. The early afternoon sunlight streams in from the openings above giving a striped effect of sun and deep shadow stretching down into the dusty dimness of the interior.

The various bazaars within are straight, narrow, covered lanes, some very long, others shorter, almost always intersecting each other at right angles. Each kind of produce, product, or type of manufactured goods has its own bazaar, or is housed in a section with a similar product. There is the fabrics bazaar, the cobblers, the saddle makers, the tailors, the iron mongers (you can hear the sound of their hammers striking the anvils from a long way away) and the spices bazaar with a tangy, nose-tickling smell that guides you straight to the spices being ground, mixed, weighed, and put into jars. At the gold and silversmiths' bazaar the craftsmen sit cross-legged (each in his own little shop) behind their small work benches, weighing and melting the precious metals in small copper crucibles over charcoal burners, weaving and fashioning the softened metal into intricate filigree work with the aid of small tweezers and other tiny tools. There is a bazaar for carders and weavers where you can buy locally grown fleeces in bales and take them home to be washed, teased smooth, spun, and woven or knitted into socks, stockings, sweaters, or rugs.

The openings that let light and air into the bazaars are at the apex of arched domes, made of beautifully crafted brickwork, some twenty to twenty-five feet above street level. The streets, or lanes, are about fifteen feet wide with floors made of tamped down earth. Usually, shops in the bazaar are raised a couple of feet above street level and have exposed fronts. Here the owner sits crosslegged in his stockinged feet behind a small, low desk big enough to hold his abacus, perhaps some writing materials, and a yardstick. When he spots a prospective customer he starts calling out his wares, announcing his superior yet less costly goods. On his abacus he can calculate the most difficult fractions and figures arriving at the right answer with a quick flick of his fingers, before you can say, "Salaam Aleikum."

A lot of bargaining goes on before any deal is sealed. To leave himself room to maneuver the shopkeeper quotes a high price, and if you are astute you will make him an offer of about half of that. As the bargaining progresses his price gradually comes down as your offer creeps up, until a fair and amicable figure is reached. Each time the shopkeeper drops his price he assures you he is on the brink of bankruptcy and his children will starve that day because he will go home empty handed in the evening. But, because you are such a nice lady he wants you to go home to your husband contented, the happy man! All the while you know, and he knows that you know, that he has made a good profit and that you will both go home boasting, you of the bargains you got and he of the profits he made. You laugh together at the game you have played and part friends with promises of further dealings in the future.

Typically, the lady of the house does not concern herself with the household shopping, she mostly shops for personal items which are usually purchased from visiting street vendors. Household shopping is done by the man of the house or, as in our case, since Papa is so busy or out of town a lot, by an agent of the household. Our extended family unit is so large that supplies must be purchased in bulk quantities. A lady would rather die than be seen at the greengrocers, and no one would buy just one pound of grapes lest people think that they have a small household and employ no servants!

We complete our shopping, having been amused by all the bargaining and flowery compliments. Homer and Willie bought some balloons, which are actually inflated sheep's bladders scrubbed clean, some knuckle bones to play *besh dash* (a game like tossing dice) and beautiful, bouncy string balls. I have several strands of beads around my neck and rings on my fingers. I feel quite beautiful, having already forgotten about the iodine stains. I also bought assorted ribbons for my little sisters and a hand-crafted varnished box painted red, blue, and green in abstract design. The box is a No-Ruz specialty containing the traditional seven varieties of salted nuts and seeds, or plain dried fruits and seven varieties of almond meal stuffed dried fruits, toasted almonds, and other things all artfully arranged. Though No-Ruz is over, there are still a few boxes left being sold at bargain prices. But, we mustn't tarry. Prayer time is fast approaching and we want to visit the *maidan* (town square) to see if the Story Teller has returned from his long winter hibernation, weaving spells over the eager audience.

# The Storyteller

We are delighted to see that the Story Teller sits in his usual spot, cross-legged on his magic carpet, his wide black cloak, the abba, neatly gathered around him. The click, click, click of large amber worry beads he is thumbing in the absolute quiet adds to the intensity of the moment, for he is at his story's end, and his sense of drama and theatrical climax is impeccable. Dark eyes set in a thin ascetic face give him a dreamy, faraway look, as if in spirit he lives in that mysterious land beyond the horizon where the heroes and *houris* (heavenly virgins) of his stories dwell. For a few moments he sits quietly absorbed in his thoughts, gently smoothing his flowing white beard. Gradually, he detaches himself from the land of fantasy and slowly returns to earth. Lifting his eyes, he gives the noisily appreciative crowd a sweet smile of thanks. Blessings are exchanged, more coins are tossed into an already overflowing bowl, and more sharbat with crushed walnut and mint leaves is served all around. Refreshments are provided by the wealthy homeowner in whose sheltered doorway the story teller has been sitting.

As the crowd disperses, the ethnic or religious orientation of the spectators is obvious by their attire. Muslim women are veiled and the Christians are in more or less European or Russian style clothing. Younger well-to-do Christian women are in neat ankle length suits and flowery hats, while the older ones wear traditional kerchiefs, or long white lace triangles that hang down their backs. The lace head-cover is worn over a two-inch wide velvet coronet giving a flat appearance to the top of their heads. The two short ends of the triangular veil hang over the shoulders framing their faces in a most flattering manner covering, yet showing off, two thick and glossy sausage curls of shoulder length. There is a jeweled clasp on the coronet, sometimes laden with gold coins. In times of prosperity more gold coins are added to the coronet, or to the gold chain around their neck, and bracelets. The number of coins and gold items worn by a woman displays the family's economic status and because conventional banks are not trusted, a woman becomes her husband's personal walking bank. In lean years, or as the need arises, coins are taken off one by one to pay expenses.

Some Muslim men from an Azerbaijani Turkish sect wear a red fez with a long black tassel that swings jauntily as they walk, or is propelled by the wind. Jews are distinguished by their tall conical hats and long, black, unhennaed beards. Today they are looking cautious as they desperately want to avoid the attention of Christians. Tomorrow is Good Friday and some of our so called "good" Christians will be out early, hunting for Jews. When they find one they will beat him to within an inch of his life, as they believe Jews were responsible for the death of Christ. This theory does not hold water theologically, of course, but literal interpretation of any holy book can lead people to fanatical behavior. There are three Jewish families in our neighborhood who shelter with us every Good Friday. They arrive before sunrise and leave after dusk, assuring their safety from these few "good" Christians.

No bazaar scene is complete without water carriers hauling goatskins full of water for catering to the thirsty; or haulers transporting bundle-loads of goods on their backs; or heavily laden donkeys and carts; and huge balls of brush, used for fuel, that almost entirely fill the width of the street, standing higher than the tallest man. The walking balls seem to have a life of their own. In the jostling crowd people are yelling and hurling curses at the passing bundle while clinging to their own piece of wall. I once experimented with some of these rich, long, descriptive, picturesque swear words only to have them knocked smartly out of me when I tried them out in the presence of my puritanical parents. I have not used a swear word since.

When the ball comes abreast, being small, I can see between the legs of people in front of me and discover that the brush is not really alive after all. It is a poor donkey so heavily loaded that nothing of the animal is visible except its long doleful head and upstanding ears.

As soon as we get home Agnes and Angel come running to greet us. They are delighted with the gifts we have brought them from the world outside of our courtyard. There are ribbons, sweets, hand-carved and painted wooden dolls, which can be manipulated into funny contortions by long dangling strings, and various other treats. To crown our day, a messenger has delivered a letter from Papa telling us that he will be coming home on Saturday.

Papa arrives home safely from Kurdistan looking very tired with many tales to tell about fighting between the tribes. On his way back whenever people heard that "The Doctor" was passing through, they showered him with gifts and money, begging him to stay and treat their ill. Among the many health problems he treated was trachoma, a contagious and chronic bacterial eye infection that can lead to blindness. The common folk treatment for this rampant disease is a hollyhock concoction, which leaves a red or purple hue around the eyes.

The Kurdish Agha's wife has sent Mama a bolt of plum colored velvet. It is sure to be contraband, as smuggling is a thriving business in Kurdistan. But Papa could not refuse to accept the gift even if he suspected its source, because that would be considered an insult and wars between the tribes have started with less cause. Papa treated the Agha's son who was shot in the thigh, and also a dozen or so others injured with sword or bullet wounds in the inter-tribal fighting. He also stayed longer in order to nurse their wounds, because he was concerned about infections setting in from poor hygiene.

Kurdish women can be very attractive. They have a beautiful upright carriage, straight backs with heads held proudly high, and a free swinging grace to their walk that is the envy of more sophisticated woman. This grace is acquired through their practice of carrying large round trays on their heads. It is loaded with bowls of yogurt, clotted cream, butter and cheese, then taken to the bazaar to be sold or bartered in exchange for vegetables, fruit, and other necessities. Though Muslim, the women do not wear the long black veil, nor cover their faces from strangers, but may wear a loosely hanging scarf or small head roll, similar but smaller than the one worn by their men.

Kurds are not typically agrarian. When the lowland pastures are exhausted, they pack up their tents and move up to higher ground, trekking hundreds of miles with no boundaries or barriers to stop them. I witnessed one of the last Kurdish seasonal migrations in the mountains of Hamadan. The Kurdish and other tribal migrations were forcibly stopped by the Iranian government. The tribes fought courageously to preserve their traditional ways, but lost.

# 6

# The Howling Dervishes are in Town

I have started to play more and more with my little sisters Agnes and Angel, now that they are growing up. I adore my sisters and spoil them shamelessly, carrying Angel in my arms when she can walk, or hugging and kissing them until they say, "No, no, no." I am like a little mother to them, and they are my own little dolls. In the same way, Willie tags after Homer.

This morning, after Papa's return, they were playing in the outer courtyard where Papa's assistant regaled the little ones with his tales of derring-do, of murder and mayhem in Kurdistan. He told of his own amazing courage, standing single-handedly and armed with just one khanjal against at least one hundred Kurds, while guarding Papa who attended patients!

Homer appeared, running as fast as his legs could carry him, Willie following closely, panting excitedly and yelling at the top of his voice, "Mama, Mama, guess what? The Dervishes have arrived in town. I saw two of them. They will be in the maidan this afternoon. Can we go see them, please can we go?"

"I want to go, too. Homer will look after me and hold my hand," cries Willie.

"Me too, me too," Agnes pipes in.

Dervishes are friars of the Sufi Way, calling themselves "People of the Path" and "Seekers after Truth." Sufism is a denomination of Islam that emphasizes a personal relationship with God, encourages mystical awakening, and rejects rigid rules concerning daily life. Through the constant unselfish practices of humanly love, meditative contemplation, prayer, and strenuous exercise, such as the Dance, they seek spiritual perfection and oneness with God. After twelve years of unremitting effort, they may be considered worthy to be accepted into the Brotherhood of the Sufis who say that they are on a journey, or a series of journeys, to perfection, to the creation of the perfect man in perfect attunement with the Divine.

Sufis revere Jesus without accepting his divinity. Though they are strictly Muslim, they base some of their beliefs on the actions and messages of Jesus, which have come down to them through traditional Eastern customs predating Islam. In their monasteries they retain the master and disciple system of teaching, just as it was in the time of Christ. For this reason they are accused of being heretics, lapsed Christians. In turn, they accuse Christians of being lost to The Path and The Truth, of which Jesus was The Master.

Among the ranks of the Sufis there are great thinkers, philosophers, and writers, such as Jalalud' din Rumi, and Hafez who have influenced Western thought for hundreds of years. My admiration for the brotherhood has grown over the years as I have learned more about them. This is in such contrast to the fear I felt in the ignorance of my childhood. As a child,chills ran up and down my spine, because for me Howling Dervishes, as we called them, were the stuff of nightmares. I often had frightening dreams about them and woke up shivering. In my dreams I did not see them clearly, for they were shrouded in a dark menacing cloud, but I knew who they were. In dreams it was their intention to chase me and to grab me from behind, carrying me off to the dark place from whence they came. My heart would pound, I couldn't breathe, my legs heavy as lead and my feet as though they are glued to the ground. I knew that this was only a dream, but petrified, Iwilled myself awake lacking the courage to face my dream and see it through to the end. Regardless, I still want to go with Homer and Willie. Seeing the Dervishes again seems to me, at this moment, the most important and fascinating thing in the world.

Dervishes are nomadic and have chapter houses all over the Muslim world. We did not know where they came from, or where they went after their short stay in our town as they were secretive and the locals respected their privacy. They started arriving in the spring when all the mountain passes were free of snow and adequate for travel. The first group was followed, at a few days' interval, by others until the end of summer when they started their long journey back to warmer climes, or perhaps to one of their chapter houses to renew their faith, replenish their spirit, confirm their allegiance, and nurture and strengthen their worn bodies.

To our joy, Papa says he himself will take us as he has not seen Dancing Dervishes since his school days back in Turkey. Arrangements are made for us to go with the understanding that it has to be a short outing as tomorrow is Easter Eve and our last opportunity to finish painting, dyeing, and preparing our eggs for Easter morning.

It is a tight squeeze in the streets with people packed like sardines, and all headed in the direction of the main maidan this side of the bazaars. Papa carries me on his shoulders, while his assistant carries Willie for fear we would otherwise be trampled. Homer hangs between them on their coattails. Finally, we arrive at the maidan where everything is ready, and people are quiet and full of anticipation. No joyous holiday mood this, but rather one of zealous, yet solemn religious fervour. We are escorted to a good spot as we are very big fish in this small pond. "This way Agha Doctor, this way, please." A lane opens up for us and we are ushered to the front where a garden bench is provided for us to sit. People are very polite to Papa and never just say Doctor, but Agha Doctor, meaning Mr. Doctor, or Doctor, Sir.

The aroma of kabobs scents the maidan as food vendors vie for business among the crowd. The *chai khana*, or teahouse, serves tea, black and sweet, in tiny glasses set in silver cupholders with handles. Glasses are piled two high on small trays carried by young serving boys. They carry the trays over the heads of the assembled crowd, balancing them deftly and without ever spilling. People in the front rows sit crosslegged on the ground waiting for the dance to begin.

Excitement mounts as men come through the crowd carrying rugs and *narghilehs* (hookahs, or water pipes) followed by the two Dervishes dressed in long A-line coats of grey wool, high Cossack type black boots, and tall black conical hats. They are slightly built, grey faced and austere in appearance and manner, but there is evidence of an inner life, the all-consuming life of the spirit, that shines fiercely in their eyes. The intense inner fire and rituals of their order can burn the Dervishes out. Many of them die at a young age, their bodies wasted, but their spirits whole.

The Sufis cross the maidan and sit quietly, crosslegged, on the carpets provided for them. They start smoking their narghilehs in deep contemplation, bringing all their powers of concentration into the present moment and what is about to follow. They are smoking opium to dull their senses and mask the pain their bodies will be subjected to in the dance. It is so quiet I can hear the bubbling water rising in the pipes. Suddenly the drums start beating and the two jump to their feet as if propelled by a giant, unseen hand, their arms stretched out and feet in position. There is no music yet, only silence, as we wait in anticipation.

First we hear a deep, low pitched hum, more like a growl or groan coming from deep within, as if their whole being is crying out to be released from its mortal bonds. Then they start whirling, slowly at first, then faster and faster until their pleated coat-tails spread out around them giving the appearance of outstretched wings. The howling and humming by now is so loud and wild that, to me, it sounds as if a hoard of banshees has been let loose on the world. I cannot see their faces and they appear to have only one leg, and that one is not touching but barely skimming the ground. With the hypnotic rhythm of the music and dancing it is as if they are trying to lift themselves straight to paradise and the seven houris awaiting them.

Gradually, the howling dies down to a hum, the drum beats stop, the whirling slows, and they fall to the ground in a trance. All around them the crowd looks like a group of statues, frozen into different postures. No one goes to the dancers' aid, not even Papa, for the crowd in its present religious fervor would tear him from limb to limb if he approached the holy men. As I understand it, this is the ultimate religious experience for Dervishes, the moment for which they live, the perfect moment in which they wish and hope to die. At this moment they are purged of all sin, all bodily needs and desires, and all other feelings are in abeyance. They are a pure, conscious soul, ready to come face to face with their maker. We watch and wait. Finally, the Dervishes seem to awaken from a deep reverie, for they are stretching and moving, getting slowly to their feet. The crowd moves aside respectfully, clearing a passage for the entourage and dancers as they leave quietly, without fanfare, carrying their prayer rugs and nargilehs.

By the time we wake up tomorrow the two will be gone, carrying the entirety of their worldly possessions, including a four-foot high tent, on their backs to the next assignment, their next dance. And if they live long enough, we may see them again next year at the same time. But if they die before then, I hope with all my heart that it is in the moment of their choice and hearts' desire.

Over the years I have seen many other dances in other, larger cities. One dance above all, stayed with me, stunning and unforgettable in its impact. It was a Sufi Dance performed by the more advanced members of the Brotherhood. When I was about seventeen I was invited by some Muslim friends to watch this usually non-public Dance. As no Christians (specifically no unveiled women) would be allowed anywhere near the performance I was lent a black veil and instructed to keep my face well covered. There was a great deal of good natured laughter at my expense from the mothers and grandmothers and lots of teasing from my school friends. Finally, when all the women of the compound had assembled, we squeezed ourselves into four carriages and were on our way to the huge maidan.

Around the maidan there were several beautiful mosques, blue tile and gold leaf domes shimmering in the sunlight, with tall, slim minarets from which the muezzin called the faithful to prayer. Several arched entrances gave access to the fabulous bazaars, and on one side there was a *madrassa*, or school, the center of Dervish and Sufi learning and thought. A fountain surrounded with a blazing carpet of scented flowers was in the center of the maidan spreading its misty, cooling spray, while a warm, gentle breeze carried a sweet fragrance throughout the maidan.

My friend's father, being a prominent citizen, secured a balcony close to the performance area for our group. The madrassa was to our right so we had a good, clear view of the door from which the dancers would emerge. Directly below and to the right, only about thirty-five feet away, was the sheik of the order sitting between two huge pillars that supported the many arches at the front of the school. He had a long, flowing white beard and peaceful face. There was a wide, respectful space around him, which allowed him some fresh air in the heat of the summer afternoon.

Drums started beating, flutes joined in with a melancholy melody, and a group of Sufi dancers came out of the madrassa wearing long, immaculate white robes with voluminous skirts. Bowing to the sheik, they clasped hands forming a ring, but leaving one man outside the circle. The Dance began with arms outstretched and as the music grew louder and the dancing faster, they took up the cry of, "Ya. . .hoo, Ya . . .hoo." Ya means "oh" and "hoo" means "the presence of God." The different timbre and pitch of the voices, the building up to a crescendo of each "Ya. . .hoo," was mesmerizing. With spinning skirts flaring out, they appeared to float in the air. Finally, the dancers separated, whirling singly, still keeping up the chant of "Ya. . .hoo" with voices that had become husky, and breathing that was very deep. Abruptly, the dance came to an end with no sign of the usual concluding giddiness. The dancers bowed to the sheik and left the maidan, their faces peaceful and deferential. From beginning to end the whole performance took about twenty minutes. I can describe the dance in words such as splendid and mesmerizing, but it was much more than that. It was spiritually uplifting, bringing the beauty of mystical Islam to an awed Christian girl who watched the dance from behind a veil with her Muslim friends.

The next day we regale Mama with our stories about the two Dervishes Papa took us to see. She is very interested and asks many questions, but insists that she is glad she did not go, and that she still has nightmares about the only time she watched them dance when she was a little girl. Papa laughs and says that he has not given up hope yet, and next time he will drag her there by the hair if necessary. Mama laughs too, saying, "Children, shall I turn Papa into a frog or a donkey?", as she grabs one of Papa's walking sticks using it as a magic wand. This is one of the games we often play together. We shout in unison, "A donkey, a donkey."

" No, no, not a donkey," Papa pleads.

"Yes, yes, a donkey." Then Mama waves her wand and Papa fell on all fours, braying loudly, "Hee-haw, hee-haw." That is the signal for all five of us to climb on his back, pushing and shoving to make room for everybody. As he collapses on the floor under our weight we all tumble down giggling and laughing, shouting, "Again, please, let us do it again."

After a snack we start preparing eggs for tomorrow, since it will be Easter and the highest holiday for us Eastern Christians. First, we must go down to the cellar and dig the eggs out of the earthenware jar of salt where we buried them some three weeks ago. Homer, being two years older than I, knows the whole routine. He says that burying eggs in salt hardens the shells so we should be able to roll and race them against other children's eggs without much breakage. He says that we may even win a few eggs to bring home to Mama. We test our eggs by gently knocking the tops against our front teeth to see if the shells sound and feel hard.

Because the eggs were hard boiled before we buried them in the salt they are ready for coloring. We have to be very resourceful as the competition among the children of the Christian community for who can produce the hardest and prettiest egg is fierce. Each of us has a favorite egg which we hate to bet, barter, or eat. But we do eventually eat them once they are past redemption.

More and more newly hard-boiled eggs come to us from the kitchen. These eggs will not be hardened in salt, these are the ornamental eggs. They are hard-boiled in separate baths of vegetable dyes such as onionskin, beetroot, hollyhock petals, herbs and grasses. They come out looking beautiful, all the colors vibrant against each other. Non color-fast fabrics, especially velvets and prints, are much sought after at this time of year as their designs and texture work well to stain the eggs. We stretch the fabric around the egg then stitch it with very fine stitches so that the seams won't show. We put the dressed eggs into a big steamer, keeping them apart so the colors will bleed together. When the eggs are ready the stitches are snipped carefully and the fabric removed. Everyone is curious to see what result each fabric has produced. Colors and patterns are perfectly stained onto the eggs. We have decorated enough eggs now to last a few days as each visitor chooses one or two to take home to his wife to add to her collection.

After hours of work it is time for a bath, supper, then early to bed so we can rise at dawn for the service at the Presbyterian Church. There is not a Nestorian Church in Maragha. Our nighties are warming in front of the living room fire, and in the bathhouse water bubbles in copper pots as the *tashts* (large, round, iron bathtubs) are filled for us girls to wash first. When soap and suds have done their work, a bucket or two of warm water is poured over us to rinse off, then we are wrapped in a large, warm towel and taken to the living room fire to the waiting nighties. Storytime and endless demands for glasses of water ensue until there are no more excuses left and we are too tired to hold bedtime off any longer.

# 7

# Easter: The Nestorian Faith and Mar Shimun

We wake at dawn on this most joyous of days, Easter Sunday. The house is warm and the flickering fire casts dancing lights and shadows across our rooms. Pari Baji and Martha are there to help us get dressed in our new clothes, for everyone wears new clothes on this day. Some of the Easter customs are purely Christian, but many go back to ancient pagan times. Symbolically, at this time of year the world is dead, all life suspended, but at Easter it always comes back to life with a promise of renewed hope.

In the Presbyterian Church garden we sing rousing hymns at the tops of our voices, and as the sun rises, we file into church for the Easter sermon. In church Papa always falls asleep no matter how loudly we sing to keep him awake. Mama watches him carefully, and every time he starts to nod she nudges him and whispers, "Wake up, Yoel, wake up."

The young people of the church have organized a lovely luncheon for all the members. Tables have been set with white damask cloths and napkins, good china, and silver cutlery, all signs of a thriving and prosperous community. The *samovars*, golden and silver, are bubbling with water as ornate teapots sit steeping on top. A samovar is a large metal urn, usually made of brass or silver, used for making tea. It has handles at its sides and a spigot with which to decant boiling water into cups. Charcoal or wood, which burns in a central chamber, is used to heat the water in the urn. A teapot sits on the little crown atop the samovar to brew strong tea. Some of the strongly brewed tea is poured into clear glasses, then boiling water is decanted from the spigot into the dark tea, watering it down to the desired strength.

Colorful eggs in large bowls are everywhere, and traditional Easter food is plentiful. Each household has contributed dishes such as lamb, dilled rice with fava beans, stuffed grape leaves, nuts and dried fruits and, of course, traditional pastries such as *nazook* and *kada*. The pastries are not so sweet, but very rich, made with lots of eggs and butter.

After lunch we go to the Armenian Church where we will race our eggs against those of other children, rolling them down a grassy knoll in the churchyard. The egg that rolls the farthest is the winner and takes all. Sometimes we find ourselves rich in eggs. Afterward, we play a game with our special salt hardened eggs tapping them tip against tip to see whose eggs will withstand the competition. We win some and we lose some. It seems that other children also know the secret salt trick.

Easter Monday and Tuesday will be very busy days as each lady holds an open-house for gentlemen visitors who will be calling all day, shaking hands and exchanging the happy news that, "Christ is risen, He is indeed risen!" They exchange a few kind words, have refreshments, and move on to the next household. Guests are served black tea in small clear glasses, or very sweet black Turkish coffee (specially prepared to be thick and foamy) in tiny demi-tasse cups, and Easter cakes and cookies. A man might make twenty, thirty, or more calls in one day. The men always visit in small groups of two, three, or four, but never alone, for it is not considered appropriate for a gentleman to visit a lady unaccompanied. The only man who calls alone, perhaps unaware of local etiquette, is the Russian Consul who lives next door. We children always look forward to his three yearly visits with great amusement. He kisses Mama's hand with old world courtesy, looks at her and says, "*Kristos Vaskrez*", Christ is Risen in Armenian. We giggle discreetly as we hide behind the parlor door to watch the hand kissing. It is charming and funny all at the same time.

Though we belong to the Presbyterian Church now, we still owe allegiance to the Nestorian Church as my parents, grandparents, and their grandparents had done since the days of Nestorius in the fifth century. Things began to change, and not always for the best, as Western Christian missionaries (American, British, and French) started to penetrate the Middle East in the mid-nineteenth century. Wars, unsafe roads, the decimation of the Assyrian population and subsequent diaspora across the globe made the maintenance of a resident Nestorian minister beyond the reach of most communities, and serving outlying parishes, all several days' journey from each other, quite impossible. Assyrians everywhere looked to foreign churches, both Protestant and Catholic, for spiritual sustenance, turning their backs on our own faith that dated back, almost unchanged, to Saint Thomas, Mar Toma in Assyrian, himself. This was one of the factors that contributed to the weakening of our national and cultural identity. Through the day-to-day acts of living, prospering, suffering, fighting, and dying, Nestorianism had kept our ancient Aramaic/Assyrian language alive and our small population, living in the midst of Islam, a distinct ethnic community. Mama and Grandma regularly read to us in Aramaic from the Nestorian Bible and the relevant daily lesson every evening at family prayers. We children joined in the recitation of the Lord's Prayer in Aramaic, the language in which Christ taught His disciples.

## The Five Clans

Assyrians claim to be the first Christian community in the world, predating that of Rome by several centuries. St.Thomas converted them to Christianity in 33 A.D. and from around the year 420 A.D. they became known as Nestorians, followers of Nestorius, Archbishop of Constantinople. They were persecuted so much by the two main Christian churches of the time for non-acceptance of the doctrine defined at Ephesus in 431A.D. that they left their homeland in search of a new place where they could practice their faith. They spread far and wide and, through extraordinary missionary zeal and effort, established Christian communities in distant places such as Persia, India, China, Mongolia, and Turkey. Two centuries later they were persecuted by followers of Islam as that religion took hold, sweeping like wildfire throughout the East.

Some Nestorians settled in the Hakkiari Mountains of present day Turkey, living autonomously for several centuries. Just as in Urmia and Maragha in northwestern Persia, there had been an Assyrian presence in Turkey from the days of empire dating from about 1000 B.C. It was a foothold where nobles and officials built their summer residences and palaces to escape the heat of the heartland (in present day Iraq) and the great cities of Kalah, Dur-Sharrukin, and Nineveh.

# The Nestorian Faith:
# Mar Shimun (Saint Shimun)

Nestorians practiced their faith in its simplest form as it had been done in the early years of Christianity, and as taught by St.Thomas. When British, American, and French travelers first encountered Nestorians in their Turkish (Ottoman) homelands, they admired them for their simple faith and dubbed them "Protestants of the East."

The patriarchate of their faith has been hereditary in the Mar Shimun family since the sixth century passing down through the male line from uncle to nephew to this day. The patriarch himself remains celibate so his eldest nephew must succeed him as heir apparent. The nephew's training and education begin early in his childhood in preparation for the position he will be called to fill one day. Along with him one of his sisters is also educated and trained for celibate and religious life. She takes the role of assistant to her brother and deals with the welfare, advancement, and education of women of their faith.

In 1918, Mar Benyamin Shimun and his sister, the Lady Surma, were houseguests at my parents' home in Maragha for a few days. Mother used to speak often about their time with us as one of the highlights of her life. The conversation, naturally, was focused on the crises facing our people, the refugee problem, and the plans Mar Shimun had for salvaging something out of the mass slaughter of Assyrians at the hands of the Ottoman Turks. The Lady Surma was as well-educated and well-traveled as Mar Shimun himself. She spoke several languages fluently and was in every way the perfect aide-de-camp. Before leaving us Mar Shimun blessed us by laying on of hands. Sadly, a few days later he was assassinated in Persian Kurdistan by Simko, the fanatical, Christian hating warlord. The news was shattering to my parents and the whole nation of Assyrians who were still mourning the decimation of hundreds of thousands of our people since 1915. After Mar Shimun's death, his twelve-year-old nephew, Eshai Shimun, became the new patriarch. Mar Eshai Shimun ministered to the needs of his scattered people, and traveled the world over to advance the cause of Assyrians and Nestorians emphasizing the unique place the Nestorian church held historically. He spoke in churches, cathedrals, and halls of academia in Aramaic, the language Christ spoke, and that Assyrians still speak. In 1970, while residing in the U.S., Mar Eshai abdicated the patriarchate in order to marry. The abdication and marriage sent shock waves throughout the Assyrian world and split the nation into factions. The majority, breaking from centuries of tradition, opposed the continuation of the hereditary system and elected an unrelated patriarch. The new patriarch, Mar Dinkha, is from Iran and resides in the United States.

# 8

## Memories of Good Friday

I am afraid that Homer, Willie, and I were very naughty on Good Friday. Once the Easter rush was over we were assigned some disagreeable tasks as punishment; chores such as cleaning out our drawers, cupboards, and toy boxes. We were very unhappy children.

Here is the story. On Good Friday Martha wanted to attend Evening Mass at her Armenian Orthodox Church. We begged to go with her and after much pleading, cajoling, and kindly intervention from Martha, Mama agreed to let us go if we promised to behave ourselves. We were on our best behavior, though our intentions were less than holy. We were not going to Good Friday Evening Mass to mourn and grieve, nor to confess or repent our sins. We thought that we hardly had any sins to confess, except the very small one lying so snugly in our hearts! The new boy in our primary school had spread news of a game they played in Tabriz, and we were all eager to try it out that evening. Having been well coached in our individual parts, we were ready to go.

As soon as Mama said, "Yes," we gave each other knowing looks and scattered to different parts of the house to collect the necessary tools for our mission. First we found three empty matchboxes, three needles each threaded with black thread, and three pairs of small toy box scissors. We each tied a knot at the end of our thread and put it in a matchbox with the knotted end dangling a couple of inches on the outside, and the needle safely on top of a cushion of long thread inside so it would come out easily in the dark. We put the boxes and scissors in our pockets and waited for Martha to change into her church clothes.

We hardly recognised Martha when she came in. She was dressed all in black, even to her gloves. Her head and shoulders were wrapped in a

50

voluminous shawl. Looking like all doom and gloom, she had a face to match. She was so unlike our jolly, rosy Martha, always bursting with vitality and bubbling with laughter, especially when Pari Baji was not around. Suppressing our giggles at a quelling look from Mama, we put on long faces suited for the occasion, made a quick check in our pockets for the scissors and matchbox, and we were on our way.

Out on the streets other black-clad women, some with children in tow, headed in the direction of the church at the end of our street. We exchanged nods and knowing looks with our friends, but stayed close to our elders demonstrating suitable gravity and decorum. Outside the church it was dark. Inside, though, every candle on the alter was lit and the glowing chandeliers overhead turned night into day. Paintings of icons, saints known and unknown, scenes of creation and hell covered the ceiling and walls, darkened with the soot and grease from candle offerings of a century.

The candles flickering in front of each saint cast peculiar dancing shadows making their faces seem alive. Wanting something to do, I started making faces at the icons and discovered that by narrowing my eyes almost shut and moving my head from side to side I could make the saints pull funny, unsaintly faces back at me in the flickering light, or bobble their haloes smiling wickedly crooked smiles. Willie and Homer were soon at it too, as were all the other children around us.

There were no pews in Orthodox churches so worshippers stood shoulder to shoulder in a jumbled mass, and on occasions like this they laughed, exchange gossip, came and went as they pleased, and shuffled with the movement of the crowd. Few, if any, payed attention to the service.

The priests' chanting got louder, and the smell of incense became overpowering. Women began to moan and lament, beating their breasts in mourning. Suddenly, we heard a bang, a crash, and a great rending sound as all the candles went out, with the exception of a few here and there allowing a minimum of light. The lamentations and grief stricken shrieks rose to a crescendo, with the breast beating keeping a rythmic tempo. Professional mourners led the chanting about Christ's suffering as the remaining women responded by wailing and moaning their grief.

51

After the first onslaught of sorrowful outcries we retrieved matchbox and scissors from pockets and quickly got to work, each in our chosen spot. We pulled two skirts together, then stitch, stitch, snip, leaving enough thread-end dangling so that the stitches would not part too easily. Then on to the next skirt. In the cacophony of the breast-beating and lamentations, which some of the women seemed to be enjoying very much, no one took notice of our activities. Soon, almost everyone in the church was stitched together, back to front, side to side. The unstitched people became trapped in the maze of stitched together flowing skirts. Although warned of the danger, I nearly got caught in a trap of my own making. But I managed to free myself by climbing over and under stitched skirts, finding my way to one of the exit doors where Homer, Willie, and a few of our friends were already waiting.

We rapidly made our way out into the churchyard, and after the anxious beating of our hearts ceased a little, first one, then the others started laughing uncontrollably. Thinking of the reaction of our victims, picturing the expressions on their faces, our laughter turned into hysterical, unholy glee. One of my seven-year-old classmates collapsed on the ground, kicking his legs in the air like a little dog. Soon were are all on the ground kicking our legs with unrestrained animal jollity.

When the hilarity finally died down we quietly and soberly got up, all of a sudden realizing that we would soon be coming face-to-face with the consequences of our actions. Too late, we realize thatwhat we have done is terribly wicked. As we are led home, heads hanging down with shame, it is like lambs to the slaughter.

However, once we finish the dreadful job assignments that have kept us in our rooms all day, and listen to Mama finding fault with everything we do, the consensus is that it was all worth it!

# 9

# The War to End All Wars: I was a Harem Girl

Young as we are, Homer and I, perhaps even little Willie, are aware there is a war going on called "The Great War." Battles are being waged around us, not near enough to be heard, but near enough for us to see the consequences. We see refugees whose homes have been laid waste by the war, and once self-supporting villagers, in this the breadbasket of the country, are now starving. There is no food left after the armies of both sides have passed through, again and again, like a plague of locusts. Homeless Christians are being auctioned off as slaves in the marketplace allowing Muslim homes to practically burst with a gratuitous labor force. Every day we see wounded men, the bedraggled rag-tag end of Turkish and Kurdish contingents, coming into the city for shelter, food, and medical aid.

We ask many questions thinking we fully understand the whole situation. But why is it necessary to fight in the first place when it brings so much misery to innocent, non-aligned people? It seems there are two sides, the Good (ours) and the Bad (theirs). Quite understandably, the Good side is Great Britain (always referred to as Inglisi), Russia, and France. The Bad side, also understandably, are the Turks, Germans, and Kurds. Now the Good want to teach the Bad a lesson, to make them mend their wicked ways so everyone can live in peace and harmony forever. In fact, it seems to me that to teach the wicked a lesson, you yourself have to be twice as wicked. Homer and I understand this, because we have experienced a little punishment ourselves as applied by Mama's gentle hands on rare

53

occasions. We always behave perfectly for a day or two afterward, but forever? I am not so sure it is possible; it is so difficult to stay good all the time.

Papa never raises his voice or his hand to us, so our most daring acts are saved until he comes home. "Shushan darling, let them be, they are only children. Who knows what tomorrow will bring? Let them be happy while they can." In later years I came to understand his sentiments. Was he perhaps thinking of his once happy home in the Hakkiari Mountains now lying in ruins, of his "Yesterday's Children" memories, of the clans, their voices now forever stilled?

American aid starts to pour in; clothes, dried and powdered food, medicines, bandages and other things in short supply. To Papa's and Grandma's relief another doctor, a friend of Papa's, and two missionaries have come to help as well. My parents know the head of the Presbyterian Mission Board in the United States, he is a friend who stayed with them long before my time when Homer was a baby. The mission sent help at Papa's request.

Things began to change here when America entered the war in 1917. Until then, when the Turks had sick or wounded high ranking officials, they would come to Papa, hat in hand, seeking his help. They always paid him well with gold coins stuffed in small, soft leather bags. People paid for services according to the level of esteem in which they held themselves. Sometimes they paid more, but never less, than the doctor's regular fee. We never knew how much would be in the purse until we counted it. How Mama and we children delighted in the counting! It seems that that Papa's Turkish clients esteemed themselves very highly, indeed.

But now, upon America's entry into the war, Papa is no longer considered an unaligned party to be courted, but an enemy alien since he is Christian and an American citizen as well. They practice restraint, however, because he is still the "Doctor Khan" and they will yet need him in difficult times. They no longer come calling respectfully requesting, but rather demand that he drop everything and go. They keep him in their military camps for days on end, working him far into the night, but always treat him with enough respect that allows him some freedom, on his word of honor, not to escape. They no longer pay him gold in leather purses, and I cannot help wondering how their estimation of themselves has sunk so low in such a short time.

Every week or two, also on his word of honor, they let Papa come home for a couple of days, but take him right back to the camps so we never quite know when, or if, we will ever see him again. The Turks are not at war with Persia, because Persia has stayed neutral and both countries are Muslim. We think that the local Ayatollah and the Governor, friends of Papa's, have used their influence with the Turks to keep Papa and other Christians in their jurisdiction as safe as possible given the present circumstances.

It was in this atmosphere, when Papa was home for a few days, that the Ayatollah and Governor came visiting and offered us safe shelter while the political situation remained uncertain. They promised that no harm would come to us under their roof. Papa urged Mama to accept, which she finally did, after much reluctance. Because the Ayatollah's house was nearest to ours, we moved into his principal wife's quarters, taking our books and toys, bidding Papa good-bye as he made his way back to the Turkish camp. And, of course, poor, dear Grandma refused to budge from home when her world suddenly seemed to tumble down upon her ears.

## True Life Confessions – I was a Harem Girl

For ten glorious, fun filled days I become a harem girl! I am loved, feted and petted, and showered with gifts, as are Agnes and Angel. We are the center of attention and love every moment of it. When I speak, or tell one of my numerous stories, all eyes turn toward me. Rival wives and concubines come to listen to my chatter uttering their "ohs" and "ahs" and discreetly chuckle behind hennaed hands.

Mama and we children are in the Ayatollah's own harem staying with his principal wife, the Lady Ashraf. Lady Ashraf is a princess of the Qajar Dynasty of shahs. Apparently, the shah's harems are extensive with quite a few princes and princesses running around. The Ayatollah's compound is comprised of several courtyards with separate dwellings each occupied by one wife (he has four), or concubine, with her children and attendants. There are fountains and pools in every courtyard. The landscape is lush with fruit trees and masses of petunias scent the air with a sweet, intoxicating fragrance.

Agnes, Angel, and I fascinate the harem women with our free, uninhibited, tomboyish ways. They are used to a confined and controlled harem life from childhood onward. Most of the women have never had direct contact with Christians, though a few of their elders have made the formal holiday visits. The freedom we enjoy is a revelation, a cultural shock, something beyond their wildest dreams.

That I can also read and write, if only barely, in two languages (Assyrian and Armenian), say "good morning", "good night" and "I see the bird" in English, and chatter fluently in their own language, Turkish, makes me a linguist in their eyes, someone to be marvelled at. And I am only a five-year-old girl!

They can't get enough of the stories I tell them about the games Mama, Papa, and we children play together at home, they want to hear more and keep asking questions.

"Tell us, is it really true that your mother waves a stick and pretends to change your father into a donkey?"

"Is it really true that the doctor then goes on his knees and brays like a donkey and begs your mother to change him back to a man?"

"Tell us again what happened when Sultan, your Papa's Arabian stallion, stumbled and tipped you and the Doctor-Khan into the Sufi Chai. Did he really sit on the river bank and roll up his trouser leg to show you his bleeding knee so you would not cry?" And so on. Everything I tell them, the interaction between men and women, fathers and mothers with their children, is foreign to them, a discovery illuminating the hitherto shadowy lifestyle of their Christian subjects.

When I have time to stop and take notice, I see that Mama looks very worried. Homer and Willie are running wild. They are young enough to be housed in the women's harem with the other little boys, but old enough to also be running in and out of the men's quarters where she cannot, in all decency, keep an eye on them. Every day she tries to bring us all together for our lessons and keep us with her as long as she can. The women like to watch us study and gather around marvelling at Mama's cleverness. She is only a woman, yet is able to read and write in several languages! And the children, aren't they smart, just look at them. Our heads begin to swell from their openhanded comments.

Our English has improved, too. The saga of, "I see the bird," has progressed to, "can you see the bird?," "Papa can see the bird," and "Rover can see Papa." What impressive progress in such a short time, so the women continue with their flattering comments disrupting our lessons. From the look on her face I can tell that Mama wishes they would go away and leave her alone with her children. The Lady Ashraf, who rules the harem with an iron hand tries, but as soon as her back is turned the women are back again, watching, admiring.

We have the greatest difficulty, in the English language, in pronouncing the "th" sound, as none of the several local languages we speak have that sound. That is, we can say "the" when we remember to try, but being foreign to us, as soon as we say it we start giggling and slip back into the more familiar and comfortable "de", as in "see de bird."

There are other worries too. We have not seen or heard from Papa for some days and Grandma will on no account accept Lady Ashraf's invitation to join us in the harem. She is most disapproving and says that SHE will never abandon the household servants and the Assyrian refugees entrusted to her care by Papa. The Christian refugees have been acquired by Papa from out of the way slave markets and freed into Grandma's care. Grandma loves her charitable work and is absolutely dedicated to her Assyrian people. As Persia is occupied by Allied and Axis troops alike, there is no outside aid so most of the refugees would starve without her care and Papa's ministrations. It could not have been an easy decision for Papa to agree to our being sheltered at the harem. Though we are the best of friends with our Muslim hosts, the religious and cultural differences between us are so great that it is almost impossible to bridge the gap in an intimate day-to-day relationship for very long. But he did not have much choice with the world at war and the safety of his family at stake.

The invading Russian and Turkish armies are all over northwest Persia, in Urmia and scores of towns and villages all around the lake. Many of these villages are where thousands of our own Assyrian people live. The armies have been maneuvering against each other for weeks eating the country bare. Thousands of displaced people are fleeing from the Turks. They are mostly Christians seeking asylum, food, and shelter in our city. Turks show no mercy toward Christians, neither do the Kurds. The Turks have already massacred a million-and-a-half of their own Christian subjects, and are threatening to do the same here once they have taken care of the Russians. Kurds, too, are in open revolt, banding together with the Turks against the Russian infidels.

We hear there is a great battle looming, a decisive one. It will be Armageddon for local Christians if the Russians, for generations our protectors in these parts, are beaten. Southwest of here, from around Tehran and Hamadan down to the Persian Gulf and the Arab lands beyond, which are under Ottoman Turkish rule, the mighty Inglisi (British) troops and their allies are involved in their own battles against the Turks and Germans. These forces are also prepared to fight the Turks on this northwestern front should the Russians fail.

Today we watched Kurds, hundreds of them, march through our city on their way to join their Turkish comrades. The capital city of Tehran is in allied hands, but the Governor of Maragha cannot communicate with the central Persian government to ask for help, so he has no choice but to yield to Kurdish demands and declares the city gates open to them.

As we watch the Kurdish tribes march by we wonder what tomorrow will bring. They are so confident, so sure of themselves, while the Russian troops, looking exhausted from internal and external turmoil, are considered no threat at all. The Kurds look magnificent in their colorful costumes. They laughingly twirl their moustaches, and prance their horses in the sheer joy at thoughts of battles to come. They make eyes at the unveiled Christian women, and call out, pointing: "You are mine, and you too. When we have dealt with the Russian dogs, we will return to deal with you, and you, and you." The self-satisfied laughter feels more spine chilling than if they would march through in a quiet and disciplined manner.

Our stay at the harem has been too short to lose its attractiveness to me. My only regret is that in all the time we have been here we have only seen Papa once, and then very briefly. He and Mama held hands, she tearful, he tender, as they spoke affectionately in whispers. It did not mean anything to me that advance troops of the invading Turkish army were everywhere, commandeering and confiscating, and that the ex-Turkish subject, our American citizen Papa, was an enemy to them. Fluent in both Turkish and Kurdish, and with enough Russian to get by, he was an invaluable asset to the Allies. The American Embassy wanted him to remain behind enemy lines to coordinate information exchange operations, and to arrange clandestine meetings, mainly taking place by night. Many brave men risked their lives for the cause, none more courageous than Papa who must stay behind to carry on, or face the consequences if things went wrong.

Two British officers landed their fragile biplane in the mountains nearby. Waiting for nightfall, they just walked to our front gates and asked for Papa. How they managed to infiltrate behind Turkish lines not knowing the languages and dialects that divide, yet bind Persia, we will never know. Papa served as a go-between to connect the officers with their Russian contacts, then guided them back through Turkish lines to the relative safety of their airplane. Presently, it was discovered that the fuel tanks were empty so they left the plane in Papa's charge, asking him to have it tied down against possible storm damage.

By the time Papa returned with a few trusted men and ropes to secure the aircraft, a terrible storm had overturned and damaged it beyond repair. They had to dismantle the plane and conceal the parts, mostly hiding them in nooks and crannies around our compound. We liked to play on the pilot's circular, padded seat that revolved like a barstool. We kept the parts for years, possibly as proof that the plane had not been handed over to the Turks, or in case the British Air Force, always pressed for parts during wartime, should need them.

After the war Papa received an invitation from the British Consulate in Tabriz to attend a ceremony honoring him with a medal for services rendered to the British Empire. There were also medals from the American and French governments, but no recognition came from the Russians. Russia, as we had known it, was no more. The great power, for centuries an ally to all the isolated Christian communities in these parts of Asia, was Christian no more. The Tzar and his family had been assassinated, bringing an end to the 300- year-old Romanov dynasty, and the aristocratic officers of the Imperial Russian Army, whom Papa had come to know, had all vanished in the maelstrom of the Communist Revolution. A new terror now ruled that land.

We were told afterward that in all those months of danger and terror Papa hardly slept more than three or four hours at a stretch. It is no wonder that he fell asleep so readily in church. I can still see and hear Mama nudging him and whispering, "Wake up, Yoel, wake up!"

So here we are in the harem, with a most gracious hostess who insists we stay until the great battle is fought and won, or lost. Who will win, Allied or Axis? That is the question on the lips of every Christian. Meanwhile, since the younger women of the harem, wives of sons or younger brothers of the Ayatollah, having nothing else to do, are always pestering us girls to entertain them. Angel, hardly more than a baby, already has a dozen songs in her repertoire showing every indication of the fine church singer she would become. Agnes harmonizes beautifully with her contralto voice. I can sing too, but the women prefer my storytelling.

"Sing us a song, darlings Agnes and Angel, and we will give you a *lowuz* (a sweet)."

"Tell us a story, Bess Khanum, and I'll give you a *rahat-lokhum* (also a sweet). *Mashallah* (literally meaning - Allah has willed - an exclamation of delight in God's wonders), what a storyteller you would make if only you were a man, a champion of the bazaar!"

I have started to think that we three have to sing, dance, and tell stories to keep our tummies full, while Homer and Willie are running wild between the men's and women's quarters and have so much to eat that at mealtimes they actually refuse food! Maybe this is what it means to be a man. Personally, I do not want to be a man as I have already noticed how much nicer it is to be a lady; to stay at home and be mistress of the household, to read, knit, and crochet, wear beautiful clothes and entertain, while the poor husband goes out to work and earn enough money to keep his lady in servants, furs, and jewels. I feel sorry for Homer and Willie when I think about it!

There is not much furniture in the harem as it is customary to sit on the floor. The floors are covered in valuable hand-woven rugs, and bright silk cushions of all shapes and sizes are stacked against the walls. Ornate ruby glass or crystal lamps fill the built-in *takhcha* (niches) in the walls, and in the center of the room sits a *khursi*. The khursi is a low, solid table covered by a heavy colorful quilt that drapes to the floor. A charcoal burner is hidden under the table and serves as a heater in the cold winter months when the women sit around the khursi covering their legs with the quilt. Servants bring them endless cups of tea, served black and sweet, in tiny, clear glasses. When the tea is not pre-sweetened it is drunk with a small lump of sugar placed in the mouth, which you suck on as you drink. I found this to be quite enjoyable, making noises as I drink - suck - suck - to get more sweetness. However, I soon gave up this habit, not only because Mama chastised me in a whispered aside, but also because I noticed that many of the ladies drank their tea quietly, in a most refined way. The ones who made the loud noises soon became very annoying.

The harem ladies don't have much to do. They groom themselves and gossip, henna their palms, feet, and nails, and gossip some more. We have become their resident entertainment committee so we sing, dance, and tell them stories. I know only one dance, a Cossack dance called Shamir's Dance. You do a few mincing steps, pretend to spread your prayer rug on the floor, go through all the motions of Muslim prayer, touch your forehead on the floor, and then spring to your feet with one graceful movement. Then you do a lively jig, whirling, squatting, and jumping as you dance to the tune of a Russian *lexinga*, a traditional folk rhythm. I accompany the dance with my own music by singing. The ladies must like it very much, because they laugh and clap and call for incessant encores.

Meanwhile, Mama is never idle. She reads extensively, and knits and crochets, making beautiful things. The women find this fascinating and want to learn how to knit and crochet too. They beg Mama to show them how, so Mama has sent home for her work baskets. Although she has quite a collection of knitting needles and crochet hooks there are not enough to go around. As she shows them the rudiments of stitch making it is amusing to see the women's delight when they, after painstaking effort, produce an actual stitch. At the moment I can do better, but I can see they'll soon leave me behind, for they are very determined and persistent.

"Give me the needles, Shams, it is my turn now."

"No Mahbobeh," says Delgushai, "You have already had a turn, it is my go now."

Mahtab, the youngest, is almost jumping with delight. "Look, look, I have made six stitches and haven't dropped one, not a single one!"

Mama enjoys teaching them. She says they are like sponges, soaking up skills and breaking through a long-standing tradition of idleness. They demonstrate an urgency to absorb all they can, while they can, and pass the skills on to the younger girls. One must not for a moment think that because of their lesser role, the womenfolk are not loved. Fathers give their daughters names that describe their feelings for them. The four ladies mentioned above; Shams, means Sun, or Sunny; Mahbobeh means Beloved; Delgushai means Heart's Delight; and Mahtab means Moonlight.

# 10

# Harem Life

Ashraf Khanum has given us a lovely room overlooking the men's garden where we do our lessons each morning. Persian gardens have been celebrated throughout the ages in verse, prose, and song, and this one is worthy of all three. There are exquisite trees, flowering shrubs, red pomegranates peeping through green foliage and thick carpets of fragrant flowers blazing brilliantly in the sunshine. As always in a proper Persian garden, there is the sound of gurgling water flowing over rock and stone, and a fountain spraying its surroundings with misty, cooling water, then gently splashing back into a pool. It is so beautiful I, too, want to raise my voice in song along with the birds and the bees. The harem ladies flock to this room, clutching their colorful house chadors around them, free to watch through securely barred and latticed windows the strange world of their men who come and go, seemingly as they please. The garden is a harmonious place, quiet with respectability, as befits the dignity of an Ayatollah of the realm.

The peace is suddenly shattered by the shrill cries and loud voices of a screaming woman. She wants justice and demands to see the holy man. The Ayatollah dispenses justice several times a week in the Muslim community, and she has come here to petition him for her rights. A carpet and cushions are brought out for him to sit on in the shade of the trees, while the woman kneels respectfully a few feet away.

By now the harem women have joined us at the window, chattering excitedly. The garden is a stage and we, the spectators, are ready to watch the proceedings. We cannot hear a word, but no doubt we will, in time, learn all about it from the younger women who will ferret the information out of their husbands.

By Islamic law (the Shariat), divorce is simple and only takes a few minutes. All one has to do is repeat in front of a reliable witness, such as a *mullah* (a cleric), the words of the divorce decree three times, "I divorce thee, I divorce thee, I divorce thee," and presto you are a free person. Women have equal rights in this matter with the men. When a woman marries she takes a dowry to her husband. The dowry may be comprised of a few pots and pans or a few glasses and plates if the family is poor, or whole villages, wheat growing land, fishing rights, irrigation rights, orchards, and gold and jewelery if they are wealthy. When a man divorces his wife, by Shariat, he is required to return her dowry. However, when she divorces him exercising her rights, she loses everything, forfeiting her dowry. If the divorce is mutually amicable and the families connected by other ties or are very influential, her dowry is returned to her intact. But this does not happen among the poorer classes. Also, when a man wants to get rid of a troublesome or undesirable wife yet retain her dowry, he may drive her into such a state that she has no choice but to pronounce the fateful words of the *Talagh* (the divorce declaration).

It seems that this is what has happened to the woman in the garden. Judging by her chador, she looks very poor. She has lost her dowry, her divorce settlement, her children, and the roof over her head and has nowhere to go. With a dowry she could immediately find herself a new husband, or a man to take her in as a concubine. It is dangerous for a woman to be without the protection of a man.

To us privileged children it is all very hilarious, because her dowry was two *rials* (unit of Persian currency), about enough for carriage fare to and from anywhere in the city. Mama watches us thoughtfully, and picking up a much chewed pencil from the table, she gives us a lesson which I will never forget. "If this pencil were the only one you had, your only possession, would you part with it or give it up if someone tried to take it from you?" When we all said that we would not, that we would fight for it, she said, "Well then, that is what the poor woman is doing. She is fighting for the only thing she has left, small as it seems to you. You must not laugh at other people's misfortune, it is most un-Christian."

א א א

The Ayatollah dispenses justice according to the Shariat. The woman has initiated the divorce, so she has lost her right to the dowry. But also according to the Shariat, one must be charitable toward the poor, to give alms daily. And that is how she received her divorce settlement, from the Ayatollah's personal coffers. He observed both Islamic laws and both parties were satisfied. As Bible studying little Protestants, we thought that Solomon was among us.

Another incident occurred the very next day bringing our harem sojourn to a speedy, tearful end. Latticed and well secured windows high up on another side of the women's quarters overlooked a paved courtyard surrounded on all sides by utility buildings such as servants' quarters and stables. A shadowy tunnel led from this courtyard to the gated street entrance. The arched tunnel was formed by rooms built over it, a continuation of the buildings around the courtyard, an efficient use of space while allowing access to the street. All grand households, including ours, featured this tunnel arrangement.

We hear a commotion outside, donkeys braying, horses neighing, and men shouting. We all run to the windows and discover a pitiful scene. Fifty to sixty Christian men, women, and children are chained together, walking with great difficulty. They are dirty, clothes hanging in tatters and they are huddled together desperately clinging to each other, terrified. Some are crying while others are praying and crossing themselves. It is truly heartrending. We do not fully understand the implications of this spectacle as our well insulated, sheltered, and comfortable lives have not prepared us for sights like this.

Inside, one of the younger women is yelling, "Come, Ashraf Khanum, come Mahbobeh, Mahtab, everyone come quickly. The men have returned with a lot of slaves."

We recognize the Ayatollah's sons and sons-in-law among the crowd of retainers and dependants, their voices are loud and raucous as each tries to have the best selection of slaves for himself. It seems that every Muslim household that can muster enough retainers and men-at-arms has been making raids on war ravaged Assyrian villages after the invading armies have passed through. They have herded together the starving, defenseless people and brought them back to sell at slave markets, or to keep for themselves.

I am dimly aware that the women are squabbling among themselves as if they think that their husbands have been cheated out of a good slave or two and aware, too, that Mama has joined us at the window. She is crying hysterically, saying over and over again, "I want to go home, I want to take my children and go home, NOW!"

Ashraf Khanum tries to calm her down, comforting her and saying that she will send a man for Papa immediately. Since he has entrusted us to her and her husband's care she cannot let Mama go until the Doctor himself comes for us.

"Listen, Shushan Khanum, you cannot go now. We are all very worried. No one knows how long the city will be safe from the raiding Turks and Kurds. You will be safe with us, they won't attack Muslim homes."

I have never seen my gentle, soft-spoken mother behave like this, so like . . . like a fierce tigress. By now she has gathered us all around her and is telling Lady Ashraf that she can no longer accept the hospitality of people who capture their own Christian subjects, selling them as slaves, and treating them as chattel.

"I am Christian too," roars the tigress in gentle Mama, "Why don't you take me and my children, too, to work in your house at your beck and call, to buy and sell us as you please. If the Christians in this city are to be killed, my husband, children, and I will die with them."

Distressed, Lady Ashraf wrings her hands and the women around us are all quiet now, watching the drama. At a subtle sign from the chief wife, they go away leaving our frantic mother and her children to the gentle care of Ashraf Khanum and a couple of her maids. Hearing that Papa has arrived, Ashraf Khanum slips away quietly. But before leaving, she hugs and kisses Mama and apologizes for the distress she has suffered while a guest under her roof. She hugs us one by one and leaves the room in tears.

With the passage of time and strengthening of central government controls slavery gradually became unacceptable and then illegal. However, in the early years of the twentieth century slavery was still a fresh personal memory for many Middle Eastern Christians.

We rush outside to greet Papa with delight. He embraces us then escorts us to his waiting carriage. We had a charming adventure, but we were relieved to be going back home to sleep in our own beds, instead of mattresses on the floor, and to play with all the familiar things we left behind.

"And I have a surprise for you," said Papa. "While visiting Agha Wuhammed's sick people, I found one of your real live cousins and brought him home to you."

"A real live cousin? A baby, you mean, one delivered by our stork?"

Mama and Papa, holding hands, laugh. "No, no, this one was delivered by another stork a long time ago. He is seventeen years old and his name is Patroos."

## Home We are Again

"Home again, the long and fiery strife of battle is over" - Soldier's Chorus from Gounod's opera *Faust*. Although we waged no wars, and what striving we did was in no way fiery, we are glad to be home again. In the carriage coming home Mama and Papa talked in low voices, but little piggies have big ears and we understand more than they think. He told her about a battle that was fought between the Kurds and Russians, an entirely one-sided affair. Kurdish bodies, in some places, were three or four deep. Realizing that the Russians were not the spent forces they had expected, Turkish troops made a strategic withdrawal from behind Russian lines to re-form and live to fight another day. Their Kurdish allies bore the brunt of the battle.

As we alight from the carriage at our home gates we see Kurds straggling through the main street in groups of threes or fours. There are maybe thirty young men altogether, all that was left of the hundreds who had marched so joyously on their way out of the city some days earlier.

Now they drag themselves, holding each other up, completely exhausted. They have dirty, bloodied garments and no laughter, no jokes, no rolling eyes, and no twirling of whiskers, for they are all too young for whiskers. Something inside me hurts terribly, I don't quite know what, but I want to sit down on the ground and cry. I look to my parents for some understanding, but tears are pouring down Mama's cheeks.

"They are only boys, not much older than Homer. They should be home with their mothers. Help them please, Yoel." But Papa restrains her, for his hands are tied.

For the Kurds this war has been a holy war, a jihad, against the Christians. For a Christian to touch them or help them now would bring them dishonor beyond redemption in this life, or the promised life in paradise. As for the local Shiite Muslims, they are very hostile toward the Sunni Kurds and would rather fall on the stragglers and kill them than help them in any way. Here in the city the Kurds are safe, but once outside, who knows? All or most of these boys may never reach their mountain homes, such is the hatred between these two great sects of Islam.

# 11

## Patroos

The likelihood that Papa would find Patroos among a crowd of refugees was one in a million. It was only possible at a time when roads from Maragha, Urmia, and other townships near battlefields became major highways all leading south to British lines in Hamadan, Tehran, Basra, and Baghdad. How Patroos became separated from his father and the rest of the Assyrian forces fighting Turks in a rearguard action, then retreating toward the British lines is quite a story in itself. When Papa found Patroos he had only a few personal belongings, having discarded or bartered everything not absolutely essential to him. What he carried was a knapsack of medical books, because like his uncle, my Papa, all he had ever wanted to do was to be a doctor. Among those books was an ancient parchment Bible with records of Papa's family going back about 800 years. It was hand-written and illuminated in gold, green, blue, and red, by an Assyrian monk in the year 1213. The monk states in the introduction that he copied the Bible as an act of repentance to compensate for his moral shortcomings.

We are anxious to meet Patroos when we arrive home, but he is still in the bath and has been there for nearly two hours. The *tasht* (a big metal bathing tub) has been emptied many times, more and more hot water called for, and many buckets of water poured over him. Yet, he still does not think he has washed away the dirt of the past few weeks. Or maybe, as I speculated much later, he is too shy and does not know how to face so many new people. Though we are family, we are still strangers to him. Homer suggests we go and find out for ourselves what is keeping him so long.

We listen with our ears pressed to the door. We hear a splashing and sloshing, and knocking of metal buckets and jugs against each other and someone singing a slightly off-key rendition of our Assyrian national anthem, *"Psi la cama, jevankah marda."* When he has finished singing all two verses, we start banging at the door with our fists shouting at the top of our voices.

*"Hey, Patroos, akhounee, ishlama allookh,"* (Hey Patroos, brother, peace be with you) then we turn and run as fast as we can, giggling at our audacity.

While waiting for Patroos we have been running up and down the stairs to make sure that all our treasures are in their proper place, that everything is as it should be and always has been. The servants give us dirty looks. They have enjoyed our recent absence from home as much as we have and find it difficult to adjust to the new, or rather old, state of affairs. Grandma, though, is very happy to see us. There is no overdoing of hugs and kisses with her, though, for she is stately and dignified. Just the same, we know that she is overjoyed to see her family together again.

Someone is yelling, "Patroos is coming, Patroos is coming." When he finally appears, he stands bashfully at the door, beet red from scrubbing with hot water, all shiny and squeaky clean. We gaze intently at him with curiosity and note that he is well built, tall and handsome, but not as tall nor as handsome as our Papa. We take to him immediately though, for he is like Papa in many ways, including his infectious laughter. He seems to like us, also. All traces of his shyness disappear that afternoon.

After family prayers in the evening we always have reading and story telling time with our parents, and we sing and recite anything new we have learned. Patroos, perhaps noticing our great potential, organizes us into a small theatrical troupe. Proximity to the Russian border has given us a great love of theater, ballet, classical music, and Russian literature so it has become an almost daily activity for us to dress up and put on plays. Patroos rehearses us mercilessly, keeping our activities as secret as possible, until he thinks that we are ready to perform in front of an audience. When the time comes, we write colorful invitations to Papa, Mama, Grandma, and a few close family friends for a theatrical evening written, directed, and presented by Patroos. Tea, cake, and ice-cream will be served after the performance.

Ice-cream is a novelty here, and we are the only family who has an ice-cream making machine, and that serves Western style cake.

The play we perform stars Patroos as a barber-cum-dentist, and cousin Hoosig, visiting from Tabriz, plays the patient with a bad toothache. Homer, Willie, and I play dental assistant, another patient, and a dental hygienist. Patroos has a pair of large, vicious looking pliers and pretends to tackle the patient's ailing tooth, which is proving to be very stubborn to pull. At the same time, he pours a red concoction from a small bottle hidden in his sleeve onto Hoosig's chin, and the white bib he's wearing. The performance is so convincing, and the patient's cries so authentically pathetic that even we, who have watched them practice, start to have our doubts. The patient's aunt, Aunt Narine, a simple, unsophisticated woman almost faints upon seeing the "blood" and hearing the cries. After she has revived a little, she pleads, "I beg of you, Patroos, leave the poor boy alone!"

Papa sent two men back to where he found Patroos to search for his eldest brother, Daniel, Patroos' father. They found Uncle Daniel and his party somewhere behind Turkish lines. Papa and Patroos went to meet him there, reuniting Papa with his eldest brother after a separation of many years. They decided Patroos should stay with us and continue his studies until his father could send for him. But they never saw each other again, because Uncle Daniel, like many other Assyrians, died fighting for the Allied cause.

In the meantime, Papa took Patroos everywhere with him; to his two clinics, on house calls, to observe surgeries. Patroos wanted to learn everything he ccould, as he was determined to become a doctor and had his heart set on studying in Switzerland. Patroos stayed with us for two years and became part of our family. He studied very hard for the entrance exams to medical school in Switzerland. He was accepted, in due course, and graduated with honors. After graduation Patroos accepted an internship from a hospital in London where he specialized in tropical and sub-tropical diseases.

We became very concerned about him when his letters, which had become sporadic, ceased altogether for a while. It turned out that after finishing his internship Patroos set off to Iraq, our ancient homeland. We received two or three letters from Iraq, the last one telling us he was taking a residency in Aman, Transjordan (now called Jordan). He was appointed as personal physician to the monarch, King Abdallah Ibn Hussein, great-great-grandfather of the present king. Homer wrote to him several more times, but his letters were unanswered.

Periodically, we would hear news about Patroos; his success, his marriage, his growing family, and in 1974, of his death. I felt a great sadness, but it was more like the anniversary of a death, for the Patroos we had loved and taken into our hearts and home had already been gone from us for many years.

In 1949, I met Patroos' younger brother Yohannan in Abadan, Iran. He was working for what was then the Anglo-Iranian Oil Company. His brother Kaiser and sisters Bismat and Sara had all settled in the United States after World War II, safely away from the arena of those traumatic events of the past. All four siblings were living in diaspora, and were among the few remaining survivors still able to remember and speak about the tragic events of the Assyrian/Armenian Genocide. Years later I met one of Patroos' sons, Baz, a doctor residing in Cleveland, Ohio. At six feet four inches tall, wide shoulders and slim waist, he would have topped his father by a few inches, yet he told me he was the runt of the family, that his brothers always worried about who would look after him when they were not around.

*Grandma Ghozal, Elizabeth, Agnes & Cousin Stella*

*Left to Right- Back Row – Homer, Patroos, Agnes, Elizabeth (Bess), William (Willie); Front – Robert (Bobby), Angela (Angel)*

*Yoel Yoseph in traditional Assyrian costume*

*Yoel Yoseph in his room in Cincinnati*

*Yoel Yoseph with Homer on his lap and their first born, William, who died at age 3*

*Grandma Ghozal with spinning thread*

*Five of the Yoseph children: Left to Right – Upper Row – William & Elizabeth; Middle Row – Robert, Ange, Agnes, with friends*

*Grandma Ghozal & Qasha Mooshi Moorhaj Family*

*Shushan & Yoel Yoseph*

*Left to Right – Back Row – Willie, Bess, Malcolm, Dr. John Tamraz, Shushan, Agnes; Front Row – Rubina, Almira, & Angel*

*YOEL, YOSEPH. B.A. Urmia High School Persia, 1893; Urmia University, Persia, 1897; Valedictorian Academic Department, Wooster University, 1898-1900; Medical College of Ohio, 1901-1903; Presbyterian Foreign Medical Missionary to Kurdistan Turkey*

*(Taken from the 1905 University of Cincinnati Yearbook)*

# Certificate of Naturalization.
### (ALIEN.)

UNITED STATES OF AMERICA,
THE STATE OF OHIO,  } ss.
HAMILTON COUNTY,

*Probate Court,* Oct 25" 1904

This day *Yoel Yoseph* an alien, a native of *Kurdistan* appeared in open Court and on examination to be admitted as a citizen of the United States of America, and made it appear to the satisfaction of this Court that he declared his intention to become a citizen of the United States of America, on the *19"* day of *Feb* 1902 before the *Probate* Court of *Hamilton* County, *Ohio* ; and also produced to the Court his Certificate of such declaration of intention; and said applicant further made it appear to the satisfaction of the Court that he has resided within the United States of America, for five years at least last past, and for one year at least last past within the State of Ohio, and has during that time behaved as a man of good moral character, attached to the principles of the Constitution of the United States of America, well disposed to the good order and happiness of the same; and said applicant filed with this Court his affidavit and the affidavits of *Edw. A. Fox & E.J. Chamberlain* two witnesses, deposing that said applicant does not disbelieve in and is not opposed to all organized government, that he is not a member of or affiliated with any organization entertaining and teaching such disbelief in or opposition to all organized government; that he does not advocate or teach the duty, necessity or propriety of the unlawful assaulting or killing of any officer or officers, either of specific individuals or of officers generally, of the government of the United States of America or of any other organized government, because of his or their official character, and further stating that he has not violated any of the provisions of the Act of Congress, approved March 3, 1903, entitled "An act to regulate the immigration of aliens into the United States of America," which affidavits are recorded in the office of this Court.

And thereupon the said *Yoel Yoseph* made solemn oath that he will support the Constitution of the United States of America, and that he doth absolutely and entirely renounce and abjure all allegiance and fidelity to every Foreign Prince, Potentate, State or Sovereignty, and particularly to *the Sultan of Turkey* whose subject he was.

And the Court being satisfied that said *Yoel Yoseph* has in all respects complied with the laws of the United States of America relating to the naturalization of aliens, and with the requirements of the act of Congress approved March 3, 1903, entitled "An act to regulate the immigration of aliens into the United States of America," it was ordered that he be, and hereby is admitted to become a Citizen of the United States of America, and that a Certificate thereof be issued to him. It is further ordered that this proceeding, including the affidavits, be recorded.

The State of Ohio, Hamilton County, ss.  *Chas F. Wilkary,* Probate Judge.

I, the undersigned Judge and Ex-Officio Clerk of said Probate Court, do hereby certify that the foregoing is a true and correct statement of the proceedings, findings and orders of said Court made in the matter of said Naturalization, as appears of record therein; that the affidavits required by law were duly made and recorded; and that said *Yoel Yoseph* is a citizen of the United States of America.

Witness my hand and the seal of said Court, at Cincinnati Ohio, this 25" day of Oct A. D. 1904.

*Chas F. Wilkary,*
Judge and Ex-Officio Clerk of said Court.

(FORM NO. 87—CONSULAR.)

# CERTIFICATE OF MARRIAGE.

## American Consular Service,

Tabriz, Persia

Tabriz, September 29", 1909

I, William F. Doty, Consul of the United States of America at Tabriz, Persia, do hereby certify that, on this 29" day of September, A. D. 1909, at the American Consulate, in the city of Tabriz, Persia, Erwel Yoresh, a citizen of the United States, aged 29 years, born in Bey Shamskha, Turkey, and now residing in Marapha, Persia, and Shushan Shamskha, a subject of Turkey, aged 22 years, born in Marapha, Persia, and now residing in Tabriz, Persia were united in marriage before me, and in my presence, by Rev. W. F. Wilson, M.D., who is authorized by the laws of American Presbyterian to perform such a ceremony.

IN WITNESS WHEREOF I have hereunto subscribed my name and affixed the seal of my office at Tabriz, Persia, this Twenty-ninth day of September, A. D. 1909, and of the Independence of the United States the One hundred and Thirty-fourth.

William F. Doty

Consul of the United States of America.

FEE NO. 11, ONE DOLLAR.   TO BE ISSUED IN TRIPLICATE.

The Medical Department of the University of Cincinnati,
The Medical College of Ohio.

The Board of Directors of the

# University  of Cincinnati

To all whom it may concern

## Greeting:

Be it known that said Board of Directors, having been advised by the Faculty of the Medical Department of the University, that ~~ *Mirza Yol Youseph* ~~ has completed the Course of Study and discipline required of candidates for the degree of Doctor of Medicine and that he is qualified to receive the same.

Do by these presents confer said degree upon him with all the honors and privileges appertaining thereto.

In testimony whereof the proper officers of the Board of Directors and of the University for the execution of these presents, have hereunto subscribed their names and caused the seal of the University to be affixed.

Done at the University, City of Cincinnati, State of Ohio, United States of America, this thirtieth day of May in the year of our Lord 1903.

*Frank J. Jones*
Chairman of Board of Directors.

*Daniel Laurence*
Clerk of Board of Directors.

*Charles W. Dabney*
President of the University.

P. S. Conner M.D. LLD. Chir. Prof.
Thad A. Reamy M.D. Gyn. Clin. Prof.
Chauncey D. Palmer M.D. Prof. Gynecology and Clinical Gynecology
J. Finley ___ Mat. Med. Prof.
Joseph Ransohoff M.D. F.R.C.S. Chir. Prof.
B. K. Rachford M.D. Pediatrics.
Allen C. Post M.D. Med. Med. & Therapeut. Prof.
E. Gustav Zinke M.D. Prof. Obstet.
A. Ravogli A.M. M.D. Prof. Derm. & Syph.

S. Lee Ayres M.D. Prof. Ophthl.
Albert P. Phelps M.D. Prof. Anatomy, Secretary
W. J. Crane B.S. M.D. Prof. Chemistry
N. J. Wallace B.S. M.D. Prof. Pathology
___ Prof. Genito Urinary Diseases
Brooke F. Beck M.D. Prof. Mental Diseases
Albert P. Bailey M.D. Prof. Medical Surg.
D. R. Blakeslee M.D. Prof. Otology, Rhinology, Laryngology.

# 12

## Papa

"*The older I became, the more the fantasy of a new life grew deep in my heart that was fascinated by the civilization and development of America. I became drunk with thoughts of that country and the waves of its civilization, which had reached the valleys of Urmia. Its breeze blew over the mountains of Kurdistan, to the narrow and beautiful Baz valley where lay all my wishes and hopes for it.*"

Entry from the journal of Dr. Yoel Yoseph

Papa was born in June of 1878, in the tribal region of Baz in the Hakkiari Mountains of southeastern Turkey. There were five main Assyrian clans in the Hakkiari region. They were the Baz (Papa's clan), Gavar, Djiloo, Tkhouma, and Tiari. Four of the clans had hereditary chieftains called *maliks*, a term derived from the Assyrian word *malka*, meaning king. The fifth clan, Baz, had elected maliks. More often than not one member of Papa's family was elected malik of the Baznai, or people of Baz.

The Baz (meaning hawk) Tribe consisted of thirteen villages that were governed by the elected leader who was chosen every three years. A story passed down for generations in our family claims that the Baz were descended from the Assyrian king Sennacherib. It is said that Sennacherib's sons attempted to assassinate him during a coup upon their father's regime, but failed. The sons and their retinues escaped to the northern reaches of Mesopotamia into the Hakkiari Mountains permanently settling there. Traditionally, Assyrian kings were considered the chief priests of their kingdoms so, even after our people's conversion to Christianity we continued the practice of the eldest son entering the priesthood, or ministry as it later became.

Papa's father, Yoseph, was from an old Assyrian family of priests and elected maliks, and his mother Bassa, was a niece of Mar Binyamin Shimun XXI, patriarch of the Assyrian Church of the East. One of Bassa's sisters was the mother of General Agha Petros, the renowned commander of the Assyrian forces in Persia during World War I. Bassa earned her name from her order of birth; she was the twelfth daughter born to her parents. In the Assyrian language the word *bassa* means enough!

Papa was the sixth and last child of Yoseph and Bassa. He was born with a twin sister who died one year after their birth. The eldest son, Daniel, became a minister, true to family tradition, but there is little information available about the other four children. Their names were Jandar, Zia, Mansur, and Mariam. It is likely that they were all victims of the Ottoman pogroms of Christians.

Life in the Hakkiari Mountain valleys was full of hardships. The Baznai had to protect themselves against the harsh winter climate, wild animals, and marauding brigands. The mountainous topography did not lend itself to cultivation of many crops, though they did manage to grow potatoes and some wheat. Papa's journal describes his beautiful valley as having vineyards, olive trees, and many blackberry shrubs.

The Baznai were also known to be artisans, weavers of fine linen fabrics, which they would have used personally and for trade. Most households kept some livestock as an essential source of fur, food, or trade. As a boy Papa tended the small family flock of sheep and goats. It was in this atmosphere, a young boy able to reflect while working in quietude, that the breeze of curiosity and longing for adventure blew over his receptive heart and mind.

When Western influence reached remote Baz, Yoseph and Bassa's children had the opportunity to get an American education. Papa was thoroughly smitten with his studies and became eager to excel in his lessons, all the while dreaming of going to America to study medicine. After completing primary studies in Baz, Daniel and Yoel were sent to boarding school in Urmia, Persia, where the American Presbyterian Mission had established schools, including a college and seminary.

The trip to Persia was a dangerous one, for the boys had to trek challenging landscapes that were more suited to mountain goats, as they proceeded into hostile Turkish and Kurdish territories. For protection from the Kurds they relied on a traditional system of barter with Kurdish guides, trading gold for safe conduct through the treacherous mountainous terrain. Turks used a different arrangement called the hostage system. Powerful and prominent Turkish officials sold the services of their sons, usually the offspring of secondary wives or concubines, as hostages in exchange for safe passage for the travelers. Failure to honor the contract meant that the hostage would be killed or kept as a slave. The hostage system was widespread throughout Turkey and Persia. It was very lucrative for the hostage family and indispensable for travelers, considering the prevailing conditions. The boys journeyed on horseback across the high mountains, safely reaching Urmia in about a week's time.

Daniel attended the Presbyterian seminary, carrying on the family tradition of the eldest, while Yoel graduated from high school in 1893, and college in 1897. With fifty *toumans* (about $150 in U.S. funds at the time) in his pocket Papa traveled north through Russia, to Germany, and from there embarked on a ship to America, landing at Ellis Island. Being healthy and strong, he managed to find work gardening for a wealthy family. As his employers got to know him better they realized he was an intelligent, educated young man working to earn enough money to achieve his lifelong dream. They helped arrange his entry into Wooster College in Cincinnati, Ohio, in 1898, and by 1900, he graduated with top honors as valedictorian of his class.

In 1901, Papa enrolled in the Medical College of Ohio, which is now part of the University of Cincinnati. While at medical school he won several scholarships, and so came to the notice of an elderly lady who had endowed one of the scholarships. A friendship sprang between the two, a young man homesick for his family half a world away, and a dying woman who found a substitute for her long lost only child. She encouraged Papa's plan to return to Turkey to serve his own people. When she died a few years later, among her smaller bequests was a generous one for Papa to help him achieve his ambition. His dreams were finally achieved in 1905, when he received his medical degree as well as United States citizenship. Papa had one more obligation to fulfill before going home. He completed a two-year residency requirement specializing in surgery, and passed the medical board exams to officially become Dr. Yoel Yoseph.

Dr. Yoseph returned to Constantinople, which was changed to Istanbul in 1930, with the intention of taking the medical board exams there allowing him to practice medicine in Turkey. Because he had received scholarships from the Presbyterian Mission he would be practicing as a medical missionary in his native territory of Kurdistan. At that time Armenians were being persecuted in Turkey, and being Christian, Papa was suspected of being Armenian and was immediately arrested and jailed. He told the authorities he was Assyrian, coming from an independent Hakkiari mountain tribe, so they allowed him to send a message to the Assyrian Patriarch Mar Shimun. The Patriarch's personal envoy arrived in Constantinople after about a month to have Papa released. He was released, passed his medical board exams and became licensed to practice medicine in Turkey. At last, he was ready to go back home.

## Return to Baz

Dr. Yoseph hired two horses, a pack mule, and the services of a muleteer and set out early one morning hoping to make it to his village in the mountains in two days' time. Right from the start he was aware of two men, members of the secret police he suspected, dogging his every step. He decided to ignore them as it would be a futile attempt to shake them off. After all, he was just a doctor on his way home to serve his community and had entered the country legally. The journey was without incident and the presence of the secret police was probably helpful in warding off other would-be troublemakers.

On the morning of the third day as he neared Baz, he became aware of a small, inquisitive crowd building up behind him, the two secret police keeping them at a distance. He turned, saluted them, and pressed on knowing full well that he would not stand a chance if the crowd's mood suddenly turned against him. Then it dawned on him that because he carried an American passport the secret police were there not to harass or kill him, but to prevent an incident such as he had feared. Comforted by the thought he carried on, the crowd behind him becoming gradually quieter, almost subdued. He wondered why.

Strange, he thought, that there was no lookout from his village to give warning of approaching strangers; no Assyrian shepherd tending his flock and withdrawing to safety, giving the alarm signal on his reed flute. And why was the crow's nest towering over his village, always manned, standing empty and ominously silent? With mounting feelings of foreboding, he hurried on.

To compose himself he tried to think of the many times he had trampled the craggy slopes leading to the crow's nest to chat with the lookout, or to gaze at the astonishing views across incalculable distances to the end of the world. How he had longed to be a hawk and soar over it all. With pounding heart he hurried his horse around the bend, which would bring him in full view of the outlying gardens and orchards of Baz. He stopped, as if the horse's hooves were suddenly glued to the ground. The retaining walls around the gardens were in ruins, stones and rocks fallen from them, strewn all over the ground below. The irrigation channels were empty of life-giving water, blocked with debris, sides caved in. A few dead fruit trees still stood in desolate disarray pointing their petrified fingers accusingly. Papa did not know how long he stood there, unaware of the crowd and secret police at some distance to his rear.

Gaining his presence of mind, he pressed on through the destroyed orchards into his native village. Once a neat and tidy village, now it was choked with rubble. Everywhere he looked he saw crumbling walls, sagging roofs, and lifeless empty windows returning his gaze blindly. He found the spot where his family home should have been, his birthplace, the place where he spent the first fifteen years of his life before going off to school in Persia. It, too, was in ruins. It had been larger than the other homes, built of handwrought mud bricks, a method practiced since ancient times. It was all broken remains showing no signs of recent human habitation.

He sat on an empty window ledge burying his face in his hands. This is what his people had always feared. This was the reason for the discipline bred into children from the time they could toddle and hold a knife or khanjal in their tiny hands. This heinous act of destruction could only have been commited by the combined efforts of Kurds and Turks. The Kurds would not have done this on their own. It would have been initiated by Turks with Kurds joining in for the spoils. The periodic massacres had begun in the 1890s leading up to the massacres of WWI. Papa's grief sent him into a reverie of childhood memories. Then a voice, as if from some faraway place, called him back.

"Agha! Doctor! Wake up! You cannot stay here all night. It is getting late, Agha. We must make it to the caravanserai before sunset."

As they proceeded to descend from the village he noticed a particular gap in the protective wall surrounding it. The gap opened to a steep drop of about twenty feet down the mountainside. Wishing a last look across the valley before leaving forever, he approached the gap. Something down below, gleaming white in the late day sun, caught his eye. A closer look revealed bones. He was looking at a jumbled mass of perhaps thousands of human bones. Shocked to the core and numb to all feelings, with professional detachment he absentmindedly began naming the individual skeletal remains. Filled with grief, he asked, "My parents, my sister, my brothers, my people, are they all there?"

Once again the muleteer brought him back to reality. "Come Agha Doctor, we cannot linger here any longer, it is not safe. You'll need to eat and rest before we can continue tomorrow's long journey back."

The next few days passed in a blur, but with the help of the kind muleteer he found himself back in Constantinople and in the safety of the American Embassy. Papa decided to leave Turkey once and for all. Since the police shadowed his every movement and his family and homeland were no more, it seemed pointless to stay any longer. He would return to Persia as soon as possible.

Papa reached Persia in 1907, as a civil war was breaking out. Many citizens wanted a constitutional government to give them more political autonomy, but Persia had traditionally been ruled by monarchs. Tabriz was the center of the constitutionalists, and Maragha was in the monarchist camp. The monarchists eventually won. Dr. Yoseph was drafted into the Persian army as a staff surgeon and stationed in Maragha. He was given the honorable title of Khan, approximating the English title of "Sir", a fitting title for a man possessing the character traits of inner strength, wisdom, and courage.

# 13

# The Fall of Atra and the Dispersion of the Clans

Miles from Maragha, the fall of *Atra* (homeland), and the Assyrian/Armenian massacres in Ottoman Turkey went unnoticed by the Christian West. The Western world, itself, was deeply gripped in the madness of World War I. Traditional Assyrian lands were hemmed in on all sides by ring after ring of fierce mountain Kurds who had often made armed incursions into their territory in the past. In spite of this, and because of the benefits to both sides, certain trade routes through Kurdish lands had always remained open to commercial travel. Now these routes were being systematically closed to Assyrians. Outgoing goods never reached their markets. Incoming goods such as tea, sugar, rice, salt, medical supplies, kerosene for lamps and lanterns, were filched or confiscated. Also, ammunition used for self-defense, hunting wild game, or for the protection of livestock from wild beasts was frequently stolen.

An even greater source of anxiety was the newly burgeoning friendship between Kurds and Turks. Turks, the overlords of the land, had never before seen eye to eye with the fractious Kurds, except in times of *jihad* (holy war). Now, armed to the teeth, they fraternized in mosque and maidan, heads together, listening to the dangerous sermonizing of mullahs. And among Assyrians, one thought, one fear was dominant over all others, that of jihad, holy war against the infidel Christians.

The ring around the Assyrians kept tightening slowly, but inexorably, as thousands joined the well-armed, well-trained Turkish ranks.

As they closed in, ululating voices could be heard from surrounding camps, enticing the mob . . . "Jee-haad, jee-haad, jee-haad!" and thousands of fervent voices took up the chorus in return, "Jihad! Jihad! Jihad!"

As the Assyrian lines grew thinner and thinner, women and older children took guns and daggers from fallen hands to try and hold back the invaders. When it finally came down to hand-to hand combat, women chose to jump the gap rather than surrender, taking their younger children with them. Those who were captured alive were thrown over after Kurd and Turk had no further use of them. For many years the bones of the innocent lay desecrated, bleaching in the sun of their own homeland.

At about the same time a million-and-a-half Armenians were massacred in other parts of Turkey. Later, thousands of mostly old men, women, and children were driven like helpless sheep into the harsh Anatolian desert and made to march without food and water, until they dropped one by one from sheer exhaustion.

Neither acknowledgement nor apology was ever made by Turks or Kurds for the massacres, and no restitution was ever made to the Assyrians for the loss of green lands they had carved out with loving care from a once barren land. All appeals to Western powers were ignored and Turkey remains a valued ally of the West to this day.

By 1918, their ammunition all but gone, their numbers dwindling from wounds, sickness and starvation, the Assyrians knew that if they continued to fight, it would be the end. That is when they conceived a daring plan. With smaller groups of men maybe they could break through the surrounding enemy lines and make it to northwest Iran to the safety of Allied forces who were holding back the Axis powers on that front. The one hundred or so miles of mountainous terrain they had to traverse was extremely difficult and dangerous territory, but with their intimate knowledge of all the little-known trails and passes and their innate mountaineering skills, at least some of them could get through. Some, knowing themselves incapable of making the long trek, decided to stay and make a last stand to give the others a fighting chance to get away. The very existence of the ancient clans was at stake. Many more would die, but the clans must survive.

Careful attention was given to mapping out different routes of escape, and safe places were chosen as contact points along the way. The little remaining food and ammunition was equally divided among the several expedition groups. They packed their survival kits and waited for nightfall.

Just before sunset, as usual, the ululating voices of the muezzins could be heard from surrounding camps calling the faithful to the fifth and final prayer of the day. Fires were being lit everywhere and soon the tantalising aroma of chicken, rice cooking in huge cauldrons, and spiced lamb on the spit wafted on the evening breeze toward the quarters of the starving Assyrians. They could not remember when they had last eaten a full, hot meal. Right now, the enemy was feasting on their stolen flocks, literally eating them out of house and home. After some time it became quiet, the silence deep and eerie. The occasional distant barking of village dogs punctuated the silence. Cooking fires had been extinguished so the only visible light came from the glowing tips of *chibookhs* (water pipes) being smoked by the night watch, glowing like fireflies with every inhalation.

When the Assyrian sentries gave the all-clear signal, it was time for the small expedition groups to get going. It was time for the heartbreaking task of saying goodbye to lifelong friends and clansmen. With a last embrace, a last, "God bless you" and "God keep you safe," the travelers quietly slipped out, melting into the night, each group following its own planned route.

The men suffered many hardships, underequipped as they were. Hunger and the biting cold of the high plateau were their chief enemies, it seemed, until times when they had to fight the real enemy. On occasion, cold and hunger drove them to raid Muslim villages in search of food, ammunition, and clothing. By now their clothes were little more than rags, hanging in tatters from their emaciated bodies. They had come to the end of their endurance, and just when they had lost all hope, they turned one more corner almost falling into the arms of a Russian patrol.

# 14

# The Odyssey

I never knew my paternal grandparents. Their lives came to a tragic end in their tribal village of Baz in the Hakkiari Mountains. Had I the good fortune of knowing them, I have no doubt I would have found them to be remarkable. How else could they have produced such men as my father and his brothers?

Until the mid-nineteenth century, the West was not aware of an autonomous Christian ethnic group living in the midst of the mighty Muslim Ottoman Empire. In the 1800s when Turkey opened its remote regions to the outside world, European travelers and American missionaries and educators were amazed to discover the Assyrian Nestorians practicing their ancient Christian faith with all the purity of the early church. Mar Shimun was very reluctant to make the contact, at first, for fear of offending the Turks, and later events proved him right. But the Assyrian people longed for Christian fellowship after so many centuries of isolation. Friendship grew between these different branches of the Christian church, and many French and British adventurers wrote books about the Nestorian communities they had discovered. All this attention attracted the notice of the central government to people who, until then, had lived inconspicuously. Unfortunately, so much interest coming from the Christian West marked the beginning of the end for the beleaguered people of the Five Clans.

Meanwhile, the situation in Urmia, being the Allied headquarters in the northwest Iranian defense line, was most precarious. Over the years the fortunes of war had ebbed and flowed. The Russians had made several advances into Turkish-held territory only to fall back again to their original defense lines. Now, the tide had turned again. Because of the worsening political situation in Russia, the military barely managed to keep its desertions at reasonable levels. The shattering news of the Czar's assassination, the "Little Father" of all the Russians, changed all that. Now the army's morale was completely disheartened. Communication and supply lines collapsed and troops were left to make it back home as best they could before they were slaughtered by the advancing Turkish army. British troops tried to fill the gap left by the Russians, but the main defense fell to three Russian-trained Assyrian battalions led by General Agha Petros, Papa's cousin, and David of the Mar Shimun family, and another fifty thousand Armenian troops under generals Andranik Pasha and Nazargegoff. The Assyrian troops were no match for the numerically stronger and better armed Turks, especially as no supplies were reaching them and their ammunition stores were dangerously low. Everything, including food, water, and medicine had to be strictly rationed. In the end, it once again came to two choices; stay and fight to the end, or retreat for a chance of survival. They chose to retreat.

That is how cousin Patroos came to us from far away Baz, and survivors of the clans found themselves sheltering in the mountains near Maragha, with Papa as their only source of hope. Although I know that there were survivors from all the clans in the mountains of Maragha, I only remember meeting people from two of the clans; the Baz, led by Agha Petros, and the Tkhumi, under the leadership of Malik Khoshaba.

When they finally managed to contact Papa, he immediately went out one stormy night to meet his long lost cousin, General Agha Petros, and the other clansmen. Mules and donkeys were loaded up with food, clothing, blankets, medical and other supplies and taken out through the city gates discreetly in twos and threes to meet at a pre-arranged location. The meeting must have been heartrending. So much had happened since they had last seen each other. So much tragedy, heartache, loss of loved ones, loss of homes and homeland, with only a slim chance that survivors of the massacres would ever make it to safety.

Agha Petros, Malik Khoshaba, the other clan chieftains and their men recuperated in the mountains for two to three weeks, healing from wounds and gathering strength. Food supplies provided by my parents were now being delivered in a well-organized manner by two very brave local Armenians named Aram and Hovhannes. How they managed to smuggle the goods out of the city without arousing suspicion is a mystery.

With restored health and strength, hope was rekindled in the clansmen. Like a shining beacon, hope called them back to our ancient homeland. Perhaps they could once again carve out a new life for themselves out of the ruins of the old. Some of them did make it to Mosul, site of our ancient capital Nineveh, which after so many centuries they still called home. They had come full circle and to this group, at least, the fifteen-hundred-year odyssey was over.

Perhaps it is because of the frequent recounting of a story about Malik Khoshaba that I still remember him. I was no more than four years old when he secretly came to our house to see Papa. I remember thinking, "He is so big, this Uncle Khoshaba, he must be a giant! But why is he so sad?" It was many years before I fully understood the enormity of the tragedy that had befallen his people, in fact, all of our people.

Papa and Khoshaba had been friends since early childhood. When they were about twelve or thirteen years old, boys from nearby Assyrian villages would sometimes get together to play war games, or to hunt the small game which abounded in the hills. On one such occasion, they came upon a cave which they knew to be the den of "a big, bad bear."

Khoshaba of the Tkhumi, always the leader because of his big size and strength, had earlier boasted that he could wrestle a bear with his bare hands. Consequently, he had to accept a dare from his friends to enter the bear's den, or lose face and tarnish the honor of the Tkhumi tribe forever. In he went and, before long, fearsome noises could be heard from within the cave. Out came grunts and groans, banging and crashes, until the very ground seemed to shake under their feet. In what seemed an eternity, Khoshaba and the bear came tumbling out of the cave landing at the bottom of a small hillock, with the boys whooping wildly and following in hot pursuit. The poor bear was dead, bleeding from several deep dagger wounds. Khoshaba, now astride the bear, though somewhat the worse for

wear, was well enough to raise his dagger in victory shouting his own whoopee, the blood curdling battle cry of the Tkhumi!

Young Khoshaba went on to become Malik of the Tkhumi and with the same great courage and fortitude that he had shown in the bear's den, he led the remnants of his people into the comparative safety of the British defense lines.

## The Let Down

Once in Mesopotamia, the clans offered their services to the Allies on one condition. They asked that when the war was won, Assyrians be granted autonomous lands where they could live in peace as they had done in Hakkiari before the war. The person negotiating with the Assyrian leaders was General, later First Viscount, Allenby. The British dubbed the Assyrians "Our Smallest Ally." The Assyrians fought with much courage and paid the price readily, for the Allies must win at all costs because their own national survival was at stake.

But it did not come to pass and all hopes of an Assyrian homeland were lost. A small Christian Assyrian state in the midst of millions of Muslim Arabs? A holy jihad would finish what the Turks and Kurds had started in Hakkiari in no time. Arab states were carved out of Ottoman lands by the British, one being the kingdom of Iraq, to compensate Arabs for their part in the Allied victory. For "The Smallest Ally" there was no such compensation. Mesopotamia was no more. Since then our people have suffered greatly in Iraq. They have been harassed, discriminated against and their villages bombed. The media has remained strangely silent on this point, the bleeding hearts have dried up and the United Nations suddenly struck deaf and dumb. We didn't possess the currency of oil.

General Agha Petros, a man of vision and courage, who in bringing the remnants of his people out of the war to safety, had saved them from inevitable annihilation. Yet he was much maligned by some who blamed all the ills of the clans on him. As a result, I believe that he died a disillusioned man. After the war he retired to France, where his descendants still live.

# 15

## The Water Festival and Wanderlust

The month of August is here again and with it the ancient Assyrian water festival we call *Nusardil*. It is said to have begun in the first century A.D. when Assyrians had just become Christians. Their king told the people to perform baptisms by tossing water at each other. It commemorates Christ's and John the Baptist's mass baptisms. Nowadays, the original meaning has evolved into pure merrymaking.

Strange things happen in the days leading up to the festival. There are secret trips by us children to the kitchen, bathroom, and bake house, each of us carrying out a solo secret mission. Every now and then one of us disappears, only to reappear shortly looking sly and mysterious. Cook is the strangest sight of all. She walks around with her huge soup ladle and three or four small metal jugs and water dips dangling from her waist. Clanking as she walks, her presence is announced like the proverbial cat with bells. She mutters something about "nuisance" and "children" under her breath, and constantly snaps at the younger maids. The maids scurry around searching for something or other in the strangest of places and Cook keeps yelling angrily, "Well, have you found one yet?"

The missing items are ordinary, humble, household buckets. It seems that buckets have mysteriously vanished from all around the house and garden. Buckets, water dips, jugs, ladles, and vases, in fact anything that can hold a reasonable amount of water has gone a-wandering, and that is the reason for Cook's strange behavior. She wants to hang on to the few tools of the trade still remaining in her possession.

In the meantime, the kitchen staff and the entire household is in an uproar. Cook threatens to walk off the job if one bucket, at least, is not found immediately. With no running water a common bucket reigns supreme. All the water we use in the house is carted in with buckets from the well at the bottom of the garden. Every drop of drinking water is filtered and boiled, cooled and poured into unglazed earthenware containers for further filtering, then covered and stored in the cool cellar. No bucket, no drinking water, no cooking, no washing up. After a frantic search a number of containers have turned up in the most unlikely places. Buckets under beds, ladles under pillows, water dips in toy boxes, and vases in closets, disappearing once again when backs are turned. This is water festival time and we celebrate it with abandon, without inhibition, and every man, woman and child stands alone!

We must rise early on the morning of Nusardil, for on this occasion it is the early bird that catches the worm, or more correctly, its first victim. Homer is always first. Water games are strictly forbidden in the house, especially in the bedrooms, but what is the harm in a handful of icy cold water splashed on the face of an innocent sleeper?

Before retiring we each make clandestine trips to our special hiding places (our parents close their eyes to our unusual nocturnal activities) and fill our containers to prepare for the next morning. I already have a small jug of water hidden in my room, determined that I will beat my rascally brothers just this once. Agnes and Angel will take part in the fun for the first time this year. We would not harm them for the world and, anyway, they will be under Martha's watchfull eyes at all times.

Though I am determined to be on the alert all night mindful of every squeak and creak in the boards, I fall asleep instantly and dream of shadowy dervishes chasing me. I manage to unglue my leaden feet from the ground and run toward the Sufi Chai. The river is raging, its rising foamy crest splashes me in its fury with icy fingers. I sit up with a scream and, in the early morning light, see Homer standing over me with a jug in his hand. He laughs with unholy glee, rejoicing in his first hit of the day. I reach for my own jug, but too late, he runs off, still laughing. Shortly, there comes another scream, it is Willie. Second hit of the day, and two points for Homer.

At breakfast we watch each other like gladiatorial antagonists, waiting for someone to make the first move. Eventually, someone moves a chair and we all jump up and run in different directions to where we have hidden our filled buckets in the garden. Soon we are all drenched to the skin. There are shrieks and laughter, the patter of bare running feet, servants murmuring angrily while doing their own mischief on the side. After an hour or so, satisfied that we cannot get any wetter, we climb onto the flat roof of Papa's clinic, which overlooks the street. We make several trips to fill and haul up all the containers we can find.

Meanwhile, down in the street people are skulking and scurrying in an attempt to avoid doorways, hugging the middle of the street. But our streets are narrow and - slosh! A bucketful of water comes cascading down on heads from above, and as they run to the shelter of a door on the opposite side of the street, that door opens and splash! Another bucketful of water is poured over the already soaking head. We have scored several good hits and sent a dozen or more people scampering home, muttering and shaking their fists. We laugh, knowing that we are quite safe. On this one day of the year if you don't want to take part in the fun, you had better stay indoors in the safe shelter of your own home.

There is a lull in people traffic for now, so we make several trips to replenish our water supply and wait for our next victims to appear. We spot two young Muslim boys who have boldly ventured into the Christian sector on this of all days. They are heading toward the river looking wary of their surroundings, eyes darting from here to there. Meanwhile, on the rooftops and behind gates we are quiet, luring the prey deeper and deeper into our ambush. Just as the two gain confidence and dash to the safety of the city gates, all ecstatic folly breaks loose. There is screaming and laughter, yelling and giggling, splash and slosh from doorways, as water cascades from rooftops and upstairs rooms onto our victims. The "enemy" has been completely drenched and demoralized, swears vengeance and retreats in disarray. Still pursued from all sides, they vanish from sight around a bend in the street.

The taboo hour of noon is almost at hand. We have come to a standstill, and we are very tired and hungry from a long morning of strenuous activities. Papa and Mama have been inside playing backgammon most of the morning, as no one in their right mind will risk coming in for an appointment this morning. They finally venture out, looking amused by our drowned cat appearance.

"Come children," calls Mama in suspiciously honeyed tones. "You have had enough activity and must be very hungry. I have something very special for your lunch today."

We give each other knowing looks, in cahoots for the second time today. Each of us is hiding a small jug of water behind our backs, hoping to catch the two of them unawares. As we make our approach, two buckets of water hidden behind the bushes come streaming down on our unsuspecting heads. We have been completely outsmarted and outmaneuvered by our parents! I catch sight of Homer's and Willie's faces and realize that I look just as silly as they do with my mouth hanging wide open. Mama and Papa are laughing hysterically at their brilliant success. I rub the water out of my eyes and begin to heave my jug forward in revenge. Before I manage to take full action I hear the last stroke of 12 o'clock tolling from inside, and with it has gone our last chance for revenge this year. Oh well, there is always next year.

The household has quieted down, all the commotion has settled, and remnants of lunch cleared away. Agnes and Angel are napping upstairs, while Homer and Willie are up to new mischief somewhere. Papa has gone back to work at the clinic and Mama is reading. I am lying on the sofa surrounded by books and dolls, feeling deliciously cool and drowsy, thinking it is very true that on this one day of the year you can trust no one, not even your usually loving parents!

## Wanderlust

The weeks have gone by very quickly and it is November again. The afternoon, though fine and sunny, is very cold with a smell of snow in the air. Mama wants to walk to the river bank before the weather changes, and so does Papa if we will wait for him to finish his morning appointments. We walk the short distance from our house through the open city gates and onto the banks of the river. The guards salute smartly as we pass, Papa acknowledging. Although Angel usually rides in her baby carriage, the first and only one seen around these parts, she prefers Homer and me to form a sling for her with our linked hands, or to carry her on our backs. So does Agnes. Once on our backs, they hang on with their little arms and legs wound tightly around our necks and waists and, like *The Old Man and the Sea*, cannot be dislodged until they tire of the game themselves.

I catch my breath as I look around me. Surely this must be the most naturally beautiful and unspoiled place in the whole wide world. It seems it was only yesterday that the banks were transformed into a fairyland of white, crystalline snow. After that it was blossoms, blossoms everywhere, as far as the eye could see they bloomed in white and shades of pink. Drowsy bees hummed drunkenly from such abundance, and the sweet perfume filled the air on the wings of a spring breeze. In the summer, the banks were lush with green grass with the majestic elms, poplars and the smaller shade trees casting dancing patterns on the cool ground beneath. Now, we have come almost full circle with colors glowing all around; greens, browns, russets, yellows and oranges. Falling leaves shower down like confetti onto our heads and coat the ground providing a thick carpet for us to walk on.

On Saturday mornings in summertime, women from the smaller households without proper washing facilities come to the river banks to do their weekly laundry. They hang all their white linen on the shrubs, or on the grass to dry and bleach in the sun. Whole families share picnic lunches and gossip happily, and when all the work is done they take their weekly bath using sheets draped around the shrubs for privacy. The husbands join their families in the afternoons after having finished their own chores at home, and to have their turn to bathe and change into clean garments. More clothes are washed, a last cup of tea is drunk and a meal of delicious stew, called *yakhnie,* is eaten. Made from tomatoes, onions, meat, lentils, and potatoes, the yakhnie has been simmering in an iron pot on the fire all afternoon. Then everything from laundry to children is packed and loaded onto a donkey's back, or into a cart, and the families go home tired, but glad to have had their one day in the sun.

The gardens on the opposite bank of the Sufi Chai climb up the hillside in gradually undulating folds on the skirts of the mountain, halfway to the shallow rim. There, on a wide and slightly humped skirt surrounded by orchards and vineyards, is our summer house.

Running through our property is a deep stream. Across from that there is a thicket, a small forest of tall timber so thick that half a dozen steps into the trees and it looks like night. We have never ventured more than those few steps, daring each other to see who will go furthest. We lose our nerve as someone yells, "Boo," and, breaking ranks, we run as fast as we can back to the stream, to light and sunshine. In our imagination we have populated the thicket with the dreaded *Desha Bakhtati*, evil spirit wives, who are known to do unspeakable things. They scream, screech, and howl so unnaturally and horribly that anyone hearing them goes stark raving mad! Though our parents have forbidden it, the servants still tell us these stories to make us behave, and on windy nights when we are in bed, the Desha Bakhtati can be heard howling with the wind.

The river itself is the most beautiful feature of all, winding in craggy curves, wild and untamed. It is noisy even in its gentle moods as it runs over the rocks and boulders it has gouged out of the rocky terrain. Upstream and to the right, the flour mill whitens everything with clouds of flour dust rising from the huge working grindstones. Torrents of water run down a steep chute feeding the huge circular millstones that turn around and around, grinding wheat that is fed into them.

After passing the mill, the river runs down another steep incline, leveling off a little as it flows past the town walls, forming quiet little pools here and there. Once again, it gathers speed whooshing under the bridge and dashing noisily down a small cataract into the roiling, rocky, cauldron below. Soon, it murmurs gently again, singing sweetly as it laps the boulders with a moist ploppy kiss while whirling round them, then hurrying on.

The bridge opposite the city gates is very picturesque. It has a single arch and huge pylons, under which we play when the river is low, and is so steep and that we have to hang on to the parapet to pull ourselves up and over.

Sultan, Papa's white Arabian, hates the bridge. He shies away from it and refuses to cross, preferring to ford at the quieter stretch of the river just upstream. Papa knows that his efforts to help Sultan overcome his fears are unsuccessful. Strangely though, it has become a game both for Sultan and Khan, the dog, and perhaps for Papa, too. As Papa leads the horse toward the bridge Sultan starts shying, bucking, and neighing. Khan gets into the act excitedly and begins barking furiously, runs to the ford, then back to Papa looking at him with a wagging tail as if to say, "You know very well, Doctor, that Sultan does not like the bridge. He prefers to ford, and that is where the ford is!" He runs back to the shallows again, yapping and looking over his shoulder to see if Papa is following him. It is a very funny routine to watch. Mama, Papa, Sultan, Khan, we children, and any passersby all enter into the spirit of this little game.

As I turn around to take another look, my eyes come to rest on the road temptingly winding its way up the side of the mountain and vanishing over the rim. The wanderlust in me, dormant since an incident in August involving Grandma's hand and my backside, now rears its curious head. The spirit of adventure once again calls me. With siren voice it tells me to go forth to discover and conquer new lands, be queen over savage tribes, and wear a jeweled crown like the one worn by the fairy queen in the book I am reading.

It was two months ago that Homer and I succumbed to the seductive siren voices and took off to find out for ourselves where the road leads, and what lies behind the mountains surrounding the rim. It wasn't too difficult. After all, in our imaginations we had already discovered new lands, conquered many people, found maps to treasure caves hidden in the pattern of our rugs, and fought off Ali Baba's forty thieves. We also tamed a flying horse called Pegasus, and had some hair raising adventures while traveling on our flying carpet. On one occasion, we asked our carpet to fly us to the palace of the king of *djinns* (genies) to have afternoon tea with him only to find out, to our horror, that he wanted to serve us up as icing on his cake, after first scrubbing us clean. What audacity! How we survived that one is a story of uncommon courage and resourcefulness rarely shown by ordinary children.

I do not clearly remember how we managed to elude all the watchful neighborhood eyes, or the guards at the city gates. What I do remember, as clearly as if it were five instead of seventy-five years ago, is two tired and very dirty children sitting on the edge of a melon patch with legs dangling into the muddy irrigation ditch running along the side of the road, munching melons, juice running down their chins.

We had used rocks to break open several watermelons, wanting to sample both the red and yellow varieties. As our faces wouldn't fit into the melons we scooped out the flesh by the fistfuls, and mushed the rest into liquid to quench our thirst. We went on like this until our bodies felt as tight as drums. Uncomfortable with sticky juice, and bothered by ants and bees, we washed ourselves in the muddy ditch water, lay down in the dirt on the edge of the road and were soon fast asleep from exhaustion.

The shock of someone calling us with an accusatory tone startled us bolt upright. The owner of the melon patch had just returned from the bazaar where he had been selling his fruit all day. The look on his face was incredulous as he surveyed us and the surrounding debris, evidence of the forays we had made into his land.

"I know you, you are the Doctor's children. Do you know the trouble you have caused? The whole town is out looking for you, including me. Come, I'll take you home. But first, help me load my donkeys with some melons for your most respected father. He will give me many times the bazaar price for them, and those you have eaten and destroyed."

Sitting cross-legged on top of the cargo and jolted out of our skins with every donkey step, we were soon back in town. Word of mouth is an effective communication tool in a small town. You simply tell everyone you see, known to you or not, and they in their turn tell everyone they meet. So by the time we arrived everyone either knew us, or about us. We were greeted with smiles and laughter, even the usually wary guards relaxed long enough to smile and salaam and pelt us with questions. We felt like intrepid travelers returning from distant places and incredible adventures. We had wrestled with ants as large as wild boars, and fought off bees larger than storks. The irrigation ditch had become a raging torrent, and we two were heroes like Sinbad the Sailor having extraordinary tales to tell.

The wind was knocked out of our sails when we reached home. It was utter turmoil. At the sight of us, bitter tears turned to joy as Mama ran and gathered us into her arms. Papa tore away from the clinic and gave us a once-over to make sure we had sustained no injuries, bites, or stings. Grandma gave me the back of her hand, which kept me subdued for some time.

I come back from my thoughts of that day, my eyes resting on the river as it winds itself in sinuous curves, vanishing around a bend some distance away. So seductive, so inviting.

"Hmm, I wonder," I say, without realizing that I am speaking my thoughts out loud.

"Yes," says Homer following my eyes, "Yes, me too."

"Next time I am going with you," says our astute Willie, belligerently.

ᛞᛞᛞ

# 16

## Santa and the Stork

There is a large poster on our living room wall of a rolling prairie scene with a picturesque log cabin in four seasonal settings, the winter cabin being in the lower right hand corner. At this time of year a jolly, well padded, red and white Santa figure appears on the top left hand corner of the poster. He is on his way to the snowbound cabin below with gifts in his bag for all who live there. In our imagination we have populated the cabin with real folk; father, mother, and five children the same age and sex as each one of us. We have given them names and play with them in absentia. Having neglected them for many months, we have renewed their acquaintance and invited them to play and have afternoon tea with us. This clever scheme also allows us to have double rations of goodies for ourselves.

We and our cabin friends have been watching the poster closely for the little Santa to appear. We are afraid that if Santa does not show up we will not know when to hang out our Christmas stockings. Every morning we run down to check the poster. One day, at last, we are rewarded by the appearance of Santa as he flies his reindeer over the spring cabin enroute to the snowbound people below. All we have to do now is wait patiently and follow his painfully slow progress as he meanders across the seasons to his final destination. Once he crosses the last boundary we will know that Christmas is at hand and it is time for us to speed up our preparations.

In mid-December a sharp eyed sibling notices something unexpected on the poster, something we had not noticed before. It is a postcard cut-out of Father Stork carrying a newborn baby in a diaper dangling from its beak. We are thrilled at the possibility, wondering if this means what we think it does? We cannot be sure until, one day, Mama and Papa gather us together to announce that we will be getting a new baby in

March, a week or so before No-Ruz. We start bombarding them with questions.

"Where does the stork bring a baby from? How does the baby get there in the first place? How does God make a baby?"

Papa says that he and Mama have talked it over and decided that it is time for us to learn a little about the way babies live and grow before coming to us. But, as the making of a baby is such a complex and wonderful thing, we will have special lessons on the topic. We can learn gradually, in easy stages like we do our other subjects such as reading, writing, arithmetic, and English. For the time being, we are quite satisfied with their answer. When our enthusiasm settles down a little we all agree that we don't care whether the baby is a boy or a girl, but it would be nice if it is a boy to even out our numbers making us three boys and three girls.

With the appearance of Santa on the poster things begin to hum both in the cabin and here at home. In the cabin Mrs. Beaber starts to prepare her puddings and pumpkin pies, keeping the girls busy since they have no servants. Mr. Beaber takes the boys with him to check the traps and to see if he can catch some fish through a hole in the ice covering the nearby lake.

In our home we are kept busy making yards and yards of colorful paper chains, garlands, hats, and paper flowers to decorate the house and the tree. Any day now, the two Chinese vendors who work the neighborhood streets will call at our house with their colorful lanterns and other decorations, and silk scarves, hankies, ribbons, and beads. Mama always gives each of us some money to spend as we please when they come. We are fascinated by the two vendors as they are the only Chinese people we have ever seen, except in our picture books. They wear long kimonos and have one long braid hanging down their backs from under black stove-pipe hats. Their thin black whiskers droop down from either side of their upper lip to just below their chin.

Our house becomes a hive of activity, as it was for Easter, as we prepare for the many callers who will visit over a period of several days. Although Grandma goes out everyday in her cart with food and medicines

for the refugees under her care, she plans to make a surprise Christmas Eve
visit to bring a little joy into their ravaged lives. Enlisting the help of Mama
and the other members of our church's sewing circle, she has made lovely
rag dolls and lots of knitted items for the children. She has also assembled
little boxes of sweets and trinkets for each child. For the grown-ups, she has
put together gifts of money, hand-knitted scarves, warm woolen vests,
shawls, socks, and other goods to make Christmas Eve a special time for
them.

When the time comes, we decorate the tree with colorful string
balls, the paper chains and garlands we have made, strings of popcorn and
beads, red and green shiny ribbons, sequined walnuts, and red apples. In the
process of sticking sequins on the walnuts and glueing the paper chains, we
nearly permanently glue our fingers together and our bottoms to the chairs.
This would have been a pity, really, because we always seem to have so
much running around to do.

On Christmas Eve one moment above all is especially magical for
us, candle lighting time. Santa with his sacks of gifts for everyone has come
and gone, the dinner table with remnants of stuffed turkey, rice, roasted
almonds, and pies has been cleared away, and everything is clean and shiny.
There is an air of expectancy as the entire household gathers together for
this special moment. It is dark and cold outside, but inside it is bright and
warm. The silver star of Bethlehem that hangs from the ceiling over the
angel at the top of the tree shines with reflected light. We sing a few
Christmas carols, the Bethlehem story is read and, finally, the long-awaited
moment arrives.

Simultaneously, all the lamps are turned off leaving only the
fireplace to cast flickering lights and shadows across the room. Then
quickly, the adults light the dozens of tiny candles which are fastened with
clip-on holders to the tree, and the sparklers we each hold in our hands. The
room is transformed into an ethereal wonderland inhabited by illusive
creatures of light who have come to life for this one moment, then to vanish
again for another year, until next Christmas.

# 17

# Carnival: The Stork Delivers a Baby

The excitement of Christmas is over for another year. The gentlemen had their usual two days to visit the ladies of their acquaintance. The hand-kissing Russian Consul called on us, bringing with him a new member of his staff, the Vice-Consul, who is also addicted to hand-kissing. The Consul delicately hinted that his wife who had just returned from a two month visit with her parents across the border in Russian Azerbaijan, would shortly be calling on Mama with some good news. They, too, were expecting a visit from the stork.

January is interminably long and cold I northwestern Persia. The ground is frozen solid and it's a terrible letdown after all the excitement of the magical Christmas holidays. The seasonal snowfall that helps make January a happier time for us has not yet arrived. This is unusual at this elevation and latitude. Luckily, there is still the carnival season in mid-January to look forward to.

During carnival there will be masquerade parties everywhere, and this year is Mama's turn to host a party. It is great fun to try to identify people under their disguises, and very often ridiculously easy. After the unmasking at the appointed hour, there are tables laden with food and drinks of sharbat, tea, and coffee. Afterward, there is some dancing, and we play all kinds of indoor games in our large downstairs rooms. The blindfolded grownups are hilarious to watch as they try to whack bags of sweets hanging from the ceiling with a stick. As the fragile bags split the sweets drop to the floor, scattering everywhere. Then it is a free-for-all as everyone, including some real oldies, scramble to collect the booty. The person with the largest collection wins a funny and ridiculous prize.

There is no organized street marching at Carnival, but people do as they please dressing up as witches and ghosts, wearing horrible, scary masks and calling on their neighbours and friends at night. They carry tambourines to announce their arrival, shaking them noisily as they dance wildly to the rhythm; boom, boom, boom, chink . . . boom, boom, boom, chink . . . The revelers also carry ropes and willow switches as well as trays with motley looking biscuits and sticky unwrapped sweets. After our gate-keeper has checked their identities (in the case of our home), they come inside and tie the legs and hands of the man of the house with rope, offering him a couple of moth-eaten sweets from their tray, and make outrageous demands for payment in exchange for releasing the victim. Playing along with the game the householder refuses, at which time the gang members pull out the willow switches and start to "beat" the poor victim's legs bastinado style. Now everyone is laughing while the victim calls to his wife for help and she begs him to give up all his possessions to save himself for the sake of the children! Eventually, they arrive at an agreement in which the ghosts and goblins are offered some money to release the hostage. After they leave the householders are left laughing and guessing at who the perpetrators may have been!

My earliest recollection of the Carnival season is one of anticipation, apprehension, and of turning into a fierce, protective tigress. It was a still, cold January night. Agnes and Angel were already asleep, but Willie and I were allowed to stay up a little later to see some of the masked groups that would surely be calling on this first night of Carnival. Homer was always allowed to stay up another half hour anyway since he was older. This was normally his special quiet time with Papa and Patroos, when Patroos was home from school in Tabriz. Willie and I had been warned about the forthcoming appearance of masked groups, that no matter how fearsome they looked they were neither ghosts nor goblins, but friends dressed up in scary costumes for Carnival. We were still ill at ease, despite reassurances, having heard so many stories about creatures of the night. Homer, having been seasoned from the year before, laughs at us and confidently announces that he will protect us from even the King of goblins and ghosts.

As the evening lamps are lit, the house is warm and inviting with roaring hearth fires, and the table is set with lovely food and sharbat for visitors. During Carnival season the tables will be set every evening with food, together with a bowl full of silver or copper coins for "ransom money." There is also a cane basket full of small gifts for the masked gangs to choose from. Willie and I stand at the window looking outside watching for the the light of kerosene lamps carried by the goblins as they enter the inner courtyard. At the moment it is very quiet inside. Mama and Grandma are speaking in low tones so as not to disturb Papa who is reading medical journals that have just arrived from America. Homer leans on Papa's chair looking at the picture of a skeleton while Papa names some of the bones for him. It is a precious scene of father and son, a tableau fixed in my mind and faded only slightly through time.

We hear the rapidly approaching drum beats and sounds of revelry, then loud banging on our front door. Willie and I draw closer together, holding hands. Boom, boom, chink - the fearsome creatures, ghosts and goblins, grinning hideously, are shown in. Willie and I give each other one look and bolt behind the drapes of a nearby window alcove. We flop onto the window seat and hide ourselves under the throw rug Mama uses in her sunny reading spot. But only for a moment, because now Papa is calling for help since someone in the room is threatening him. I look through a gap in the drapes and what I see drives me berzerk, stark raving mad! The vile creatures have tied my Papa's hands and feet together and are beating his feet with vicious looking switches. For some reason Papa is laughing, yet shouting, "No, no, no! I won't give you anything, not even a *shahie* (a red cent)." Mama, looking largely unsympathetic, is also laughing and urging him to give them all they have asked for, even to the half of his vast kingdom. Well, I never knew before that we had a vast kingdom to give away, but we will not do it anyway. No one is going to hurt my Papa, not while I am around!

Forgetting all the fears that have sent me scuttling behind the curtains, and fierce as a tigress out to save her cub, I dash to the fireplace and grab a heavy iron poker. I wave it around wildly, threatening to kill them all if they don't leave my Papa alone! For a moment there is a stunned silence, then somebody grabs me from behind and seizes the poker from my hands. Once again, everyone starts to laugh, including the ghosts, a loud uproarious laughter. I never imagined that ghosts could be so jolly. Papa lovingly thanks me for saving him, while the creatures unbind his legs.

Mama is counting out silver into each pair of hands, while Grandma gives them gifts from the basket and offers them sweets. The identity of at least one goblin is revealed when he calls us children over and offers us each a small package. Homer accepts without hesitation, but Willie and I stand back cautiously, clutching each other.

"Come on Bess, come on Ooilly, I won't hurt you." Ooilly? No one calls Willie that except for one person, Mr. Gregorian, Papa's agent and our bazaar friend. Mr. Gregorian, of all people, beating Papa with a willow switch? I would push him into the open hearth fire if I could.

# The Stork Delivers a Baby

After what seemed like forever, on March 14, 1923, the stork finally arrived bringing us a baby brother. Now our numbers were even, three girls and three boys. We called our little brother Robert, nicknaming him Bobby. We indulged his every whim just as we had with Agnes and Angel. My little sisters did not resent the new baby and were more like little mothers to him.

As a toddler Bobby was very chubby, staggering around on his little legs sporting a pageboy haircut. One of Homer's and Willie's American teachers, Mr. Bowman, called him "football." The name stuck until his early teens when Bobby slimmed down and shot up like a weed.

Around the same time our next door neighbours, the hand-kissing Russian Consul and his wife, were also visited by the stork, receiving a little girl they named Verushka. She was a long-legged, blue-eyed blonde. Verushka and Bobby were inseparable, but they always fought and afterward would make up with a kiss. Bobby teased her mercilessly, pulling at her long pigtails whenever she let him get near enough. When he succeeded she would stamp her feet angrily and, blue eyes blazing, run to report the incident to her dear Papa. Then she ran back and yelled, "Papa says Bobby is a very bad boy." At that, Bobby became repentant and promised to mend his ways. Verushka would run back to report this new development to dear Papa and came back to say, "Papa says Bobby is a very good boy!"

As the reign of terror in Russia tightened its grip the Consul and his wife were recalled to Russia, promising they would write as soon as they could. We did not hear from them again. I have often wondered what happened to them. Verushka would be seventy-five years old now. Did she survive the calamitous events of that time, and if so, does she sometimes look back to those happy days of our carefree childhood.

When the stork delivered our baby it did not predict his future. Bobby ventured from the walled city of Maragha, across the ocean to the New World to become System Safety Manager for Boeing on the Apollo project, the NASA/Industry Team responsible for putting the first man on the moon and bringing him safely back to Earth. Bobby retired as vice president of Boeing Environmental Products after a thirty-year career with the company.

## Agnes, Angel & Bobby

After the Tamiroff's left, a Christian Arab family moved into their vacated house next door. The Saghis had three children, two of whom (James and Edith) immediately became fast friends with our three youngest ones, a friendship that continues to this day. The mischief they got into is quite unbelievable, the only limits coming from Angel who was always thoughtful and considerate of Mama's feelings. When Mama was at home James and Edith were very shy, rarely speaking above a whisper. They were the best mannered children in the city. As soon as her back was turned there was a metamorphosis and things started to happen. The two galvanized into an energetic life force, with Agnes, Angel, and Bobby joining in for the mischief.

Predictably, their favorite place was the basement and cellars. They gave full reign to their imaginations there, playing at treasure hunts, games of ghosts and ghouls, and hide-and-seek among the huge storage boxes and Aladdin jars. The jars hung from wooden structures by their bulging midsections casting frightening shadows across the floor. The bread rack under which one, or ten, could hide, and the rows upon rows of *milagh* hanging on hooks from the ceiling added to the mystery of the place. Milaghs are string garlands on which about eight bunches of grapes are tied and hung on hooks from the ceiling. This is done at the last picking of the season using only the best grapes, intended to keep them fresh, or nearly fresh, for three to four months. Every Christian family who had cellars like ours had one ambition - to preserve their grapes so that they were still fresh enough to be served at Christmas. The grapes were served to guests in tiny bunches, all the while the hosts would boast about the excellence of their cellars. It was especially rewarding if their neighbor's cellars had failed, having caused them to eat their grapes earlier in the year; in the same way a person would also boast about their wine cellar. In my child's mind, of course, wine was a terrible waste of good grapes!

While playing in the basement one day, the children noticed that the lid of one of the large wooden boxes was loose enough that it rattled and shook if you jumped on it. Soon four of them were on the box, jumping as if on a trampoline. They jumped up and down trying to make the lid bounce, yelling and egging each other on. Inside the box were rows of large glass jars full of precious sour cherry cordial preserved for the winter months. Unexpectedly, the lid broke dumping all four helter-skelter into the box of shattered glass and beautiful, blood red cherry syrup. Angel came running upstairs frightened and in tears to report the incident. On seeing them, I nearly fainted with fright, unable to tell where the red syrup ended and the real blood and injuries started. The four were a frightful sight and their shrieks and howls added to the pandemonium. Amazingly, there were

🐫🐫🐫

no serious injuries, just a few cuts, gashes, and bruises. They were the luckiest four children to live to tell the tale.

Just then, Mama knocked on the street gate, returning from her Ladies Guild meeting. She loved signaling us with her signature knock as if to say, "Children, it is me. I am home." And we always rushed to see who would be the first one to get to the gate. And now, knock-knock, knock-knock, knock. As Angel ran up the basement steps the howling in the cellar suddenly stopped. James and Edith gave each other one look, jumped out of the box, ran up the stairs, through our courtyard and connecting gate, disappearing into their own courtyard. Loud, horrified screams from next door informed us the two had arrived home safely.

CRTCR CRT

# 18

## Monarchy - Republic Monarchy - Republic - Monarchy?

I was the third generation female member of my family to graduate from an American school. Grandma Ghozal was one of the first girls in Persia to do so, my Mama second, and I the third, but also the last. After my graduation all foreign schools were nationalized. When the Americans departed they left behind not only beautiful, established schools, colleges, and hospitals, but also a core of well-educated Christian and Muslim men and women. The men were capable of filling high positions in the government and were to become Persia's future doctors, lawyers, and educators. The women, forward looking and smart, became the mothers of a new breed of bright, gifted children eager to learn and with dreams of becoming tomorrow's professionals. Persia was ahead of its time in the Middle East for having a very educated population largely due to Western influence.

Persia was starting to be known as Iran when, in 1906, Mozaffar-al-Din Shah (who had given my Grandma the nickname Ghozal) was forced by popular demand to formally assemble the first *Majlis*, or National Assembly, which drew up the first liberal constitution. Later, Mozaffar-al-Din's son, Mohammad Ali Shah, was deposed when he tried to overthrow the new constitution. As a last attempt to save the monarchy Mohammad Ali Shah's twelve-year-old son, Ahmad Shah, was placed on the throne as a regent, but only for a short time. The populace was unhappy, the country bankrupt, and the court system corrupt. Finally, after years of heated debates, the Majlis abolished the monarchy and declared the country a republic. It took many weeks for the news to reach all the widely spread provinces of the empire. Amazingly, throughout this entire political conflict with Mozaffar-al-Din and the dethroning of his son and grandson, there had been no bloodshed. Ahmad Shah, twenty-two-years-old at the time, was informed of the Majlis decision and asked to leave the country with his household and any retinue that chose to go with him, promising never to return. He died in exile in 1930, at the age of thirty-two.

The infant republic did not last long, however. A new age was dawning and Persia was well on its way to becoming a monarchy again. A new dynasty was about to be born. I, too, would be presenting flowers to a shah and his son, as my Grandma had done some fifty-five years earlier. The new monarch was Reza Pahlavi. He came from a humble background, but claimed descent from an ancient line of shahs. He rose through the ranks from sergeant to *Vazier-I Jang*, Minister for War and Commander in Chief. Then in 1923, he became prime minister which made him the most powerful man in the country and his position unassailable. In 1925, he was crowned shah. The Majlis was reluctant but powerless in the matter. It was rumored that, like Napoleon, the shah had crowned himself, an act of unwillingness to be in anybody's debt.

Though almost illiterate, Reza Pahlavi was a man of great vision with clear ideas about the direction the country would take under his rule. During his reign railway links were established between major cities, and roads were improved allowing access to the farthest corners of the land. This was not just for the sake of convenience for the citizens or for commerce, but also to make it easier for troop movement in case of political rebellion. At that time there were still some walled cities, but Reza Shah had the walls torn down so that no city gates could ever again be locked against him.

Schools sprouted up everywhere with education gradually becoming compulsory to the sixth grade, not only for boys but for girls as well. The veil, too, was abolished in the 1930s. The Shah also curbed the power of mullahs, and confined the mournful and realistic passion plays of the Shiite religion to the mosques. These sudden changes, in addition to the emancipation of women, enraged the populace. You could see the reaction in the streets, and in the bazaars the mood had turned ugly. We never thought that the Shah could get away with it, but he did, at least for a while. It took fifty-five years for the religious sects to regain control again. With the return of the Ayatollah Khomeini from exile everything in Iran went back to the way it had been before Reza Shah, and became an authoritarian theocracy into the bargain.

Sometime at the beginning of his reign the new Shah made a triumphal procession through Tabriz. There were arches built everywhere on the main streets, and our neighborhood streets were decked with beautiful blooms. His open car traveled slowly through the streets stopping at every arch to accept petitions, flowers, and gifts. The Shah was very formal and unsmiling, presenting his martial aspect to the public, as did the little boy of nine or ten sitting beside him. The boy was the Crown Prince Mohammad Reza, later to become the last Shah of Iran. As I curtsied nervously and looked up to present him with my bouquet, I realized that the boy looked frightened. The roaring crowd around the open car looked angry and menacing. But when he reached down to receive the flowers, he smiled and the shyness and formality seemed to disappear. In later years I would remember that smile and the shy, frightened boy who was a very reluctant crown prince.

In those days the British had long arms with fingers in every pie, including, it seemed, in Iranian affairs. Since Reza Shah was doing his best to pry British fingers from his country's business, he was not very popular with them either. He lost the contest and was banished to the island of Madagascar. His son, the little prince of the flowers, ascended the Peacock Throne in 1941. Reza Shah, the father, died in exile in Madagascar in 1944. Permission was granted for his remains to be returned to Iran for state burial.

Mohammad Reza Pahlevi, Shah-han-Shah, like his father, died in exile, but lies buried under foreign skies. I wonder if Iran will ever have the grace to accept his remains for burial in his native land? If not from sentiment then from a sense of history, for he was their last Shah ending a proud two-thousand-year monarchy.

# 19

## Mama - A Tribute: The Winds of Change

Mama was petite, slim, and very pretty, with large eyes, perfect skin, and a lovely smile. After Papa and us, her ruling passion was books, books, and more books. With her mother, our Grandma Ghozal, running the household smoothly and efficiently she had plenty of time to indulge her love of reading. Her interests were broad and diverse; from Tolstoy to Maxim Gorky, Dickens to Walter Scott and Tennyson, Alexander Dumas, Victor Hugo, Goethe, and Marie Corelli. Aside from the Bible that she read in Aramaic every morning, her favorites remained the Illiad, Odyssey and Aeneid, and other tales of ancient Greece and Rome. She was the most Christian person I have ever known, yet her love of pagan literature and pagan times was dear to her to the very end of her life.

Mama was born in Urmia on June 6, 1886, and died on May 5, 1966. She met and married Papa in 1909, surviving him by forty-three years. In my early teens I learned that there was another man interested in courting her after Papa's death, but she refused to receive him. I asked her why since the man was also a doctor, a widower, and suitable. Her reply was, "Bess, how could you even think of such a thing? After a man like your Papa, I could not contemplate marriage with anyone else." Later in life I understood just what she meant and was glad she did not remarry. After Papa died she was father as well as mother to us, a protector, a mother hen gathering us all under her wings, sheltering us from harm. Our welcoming home became a gathering place for our friends. We sang songs around the piano, played indoor games and created theatricals. I can still see the yellow samovar bubbling for tea, and food coming out of the kitchen to feed hungry youngsters, for some of our friends were not as fortunate as we were. The best thing that a child can have is a loving and caring mother, a mother just like mine was.

Mama went to boarding school in Tabriz, and after graduating from the American Girls' College she taught there for two years. Her given name was Shushan, meaning lily, but no one called her that except Papa and her parents. Her friends called her Tsovinar, which Papa disliked very much. When she was at boarding school one of her teachers, an ardent classicist, started calling her Tsovinar, the name of an Armenian water nymph, whose part Mama read in a play at school. Afterward, he insisted that everyone call her by that name because it suited her so well. The name stuck and the story of the nymph became well known, even to those who were not familiar with the literature. In time her given name was nearly forgotten, but not when it suited her friends to remember it. When the name day of Saint Shushan came around in September, everybody remembered. Friends and acquaintances came in droves with husbands in tow, calling her Tsovinar, yet offering her their congratulations for being named after such a virtuous saint!

Name days originated in the Middle Ages, a tradition of the Catholic and Orthodox churches, to commemorate the names of saints and martyrs of the church. To celebrate the day, the family of the namesake would receive and entertain guests. One of my favorite traditional foods served on name day was *varyeni*, a Russian-style chunky jam made from whole fruit, such as black cherries, floating in thick syrup. It was served with black tea that was poured into small clear glasses placed on colorful little saucers. Varyeni was traditionally served in petite cut glass dishes. The proper way to eat the delicacy was to hold your tiny jam spoon daintily with thumb and forefinger, while the pinky finger curled slightly, was held away from the others as etiquette demanded. With every spoonful of the varyeni you ate you took a sip of your tea to sweeten it.

## The Winds of Change

Despite the episode of the Christian slaves, Mama's friendship with the Ayatollah's ladies continued until 1923, when life circumstances and the winds of change swept us apart to distant places and different lifestyles. In all those years, mainly because of their lack of literacy, there had been no direct contact between us. Then one day, unexpectedly, a verbal message was delivered to Mama by an old retainer of the Lady Shams. "Would Mama and Bess Khanum take tea with her one day at our earliest convenience, as her stay in Tabriz would only be a short one?" Mama was delighted at the invitation and a little tearful, perhaps recalling the tragedies that had befallen both our families since the happy times we had shared back in Maragha.

Lady Shams's family home in Tabriz was set in the middle of secluded gardens with high walls and a solid timber gate, as befitted a lady of high rank living a traditional Muslim lifestyle. These secluded old houses, like ours had been in Maragha, lingered here and there for some years until the emancipation of women took a firmer hold. Then, walls were demolished and houses modernized to suit the lifestyle of the new, modern-day Iranian.

I hardly recognised Zarifa, the youngest daughter with whom I had played in my harem days. At sixteen, two years older than I, she looked all grown up and very pretty, with large dark eyes and a lovely smile. I could hardly believe it when we were told that mother and daughter were on their way to Tehran for Zarifa's forthcoming marriage to a man she had never met. Everything, including the groom, had been arranged by her brothers as was the custom.

The changing times that had taken us away from Maragha had also affected Lady Shams's family. Newly widened roads had replaced ancient pathways, and faster forms of transportation had displaced travel by caravan, wagon, and carriage, consequently opening up vast new horizons. Walls around cities and locked city gates had been breached to discourage rebellion against the central government and tax collectors. Racial and cultural barriers, too, were gradually being broken down. The teaching of the Persian language, Farsi, and education up to the sixth grade for both boys and girls had become compulsory. The country was now called Iran. Persia and the many non-Persian provinces that were a part of her ancient empire, were now bound together by one common language under the rule of the first Shah of a new dynasty, Reza Shah Pahlavi.

In this atmosphere of change, Shams Khanum's family had also widened its horizons. Always powerful, wealthy, and influential, her sons now occupied high positions in the capital city of Tehran and had married their sisters into other influential families, thus widening their sphere of influence. But Shams Khanum, like many older Muslim women of the old guard, had not adapted well to the changes and did not like the bright new world, which had scattered her family. And was now, it was taking her last remaining child from her. She did not want to be emancipated. She was happy to be sheltered and protected in her little world of secluded house and garden with its "thinking fountain," scented flowers and trees, and nightingales singing sweetly on the branches. With the emancipation of women, the all enveloping black chador was abolished and no woman, young or old, poor or rich, was permitted to be seen in one. But Shams Khanum was uncomfortable with these sudden changes and did not like them at all. Nowadays, she always went out in a closed carriage with a large scarf tied round her head and face. At home she still wore her brightly printed house chador, wrapped around her intrepidly like a badge of honor.

When we took our leave from her home we promised to keep in touch, but Lady Shams seemed anxious. She was going to a strange new land, the land of the Persians whose language she did not know and whose ways she did not understand. She felt she was betraying her own people, turning her back on her Turkoman heritage, the great family of the once conquering Turkoman tribes of northwestern Persia. Zarifa promised me she would write if she could, but she never did. Perhaps her new husband did not permit his wife the liberty of friendship with a Christian girl. Or perhaps she was swallowed up by the vortex we call life.

# 20

## Grandmother Ghozal, An Assyrian Legend

My grandmother Ghozal, born Rakhie Tamraz (1859-1929), was a most remarkable woman when one considers the country of her birth and the times in which she lived. In the mid 1870s, after being among the first graduates of the American Girls's School in Urmia, she studied nursing at the nearby American Hospital. Work and study, however, were far from her thoughts that beautiful summer day in 1875, that began at dawn when she looked out onto the rosy orange glow lighting the eastern sky. A general holiday had been declared that day as the Shah-han-Shah Nasir al-Din Shah Qajar, whose entourage had camped outside Urmia overnight, would be entering the city in a triumphal procession. All his subjects were commanded to come out in force to give him a rousing welcome. As Rakhie dressed herself in her Sunday finery she could not in her wildest dreams have imagined that she would become a married woman that same day. She was, as yet, uncommitted and marriage to her was just a rosy dream for the future.

The royal procession turned out to be exceptionally impressive. The pageantry and show of might struck terror in the hearts of tribesmen who may have entertained thoughts of rebellion. The horses, the accoutrements of battle, the jewels of the guard, were all worth a king's ransom. All eyes were on the Shah. His horse was magnificent, showing the impeccable breeding of centuries, some said going back to the days of the Prophet Himself. His clothes shone with gold thread and at the base of the jeweled feather on his turban flashed a huge diamond the size of a duck egg, so I was told. "Darya-i-Noor, Darya-i-Noor, could it be the Darya-i-Noor?," were the whispered comments on everyone's lips. The Darya-i-

חחח

Noor, or "Sea of Light," was the famous sister diamond to the "Mountain of Light," the Koh-i Noor, which is now set in the British crown.

The Shah was young and seemed to be enjoying himself immensely as he smiled and waved a bejeweled hand in acknowledgment of the loud cheers that greeted him everywhere. He laughed gaily, scanning the faces of the unveiled Christian women in the crowd. All at once, he brought his horse to a halt in front of the Assyrian contingent to receive homage and the customary petitions from their leaders. His eyes came to rest on Rakhie, staying fixed for a long time. He stopped his merriment, as did the rest of his party on cue. With a quick click of his fingers he summoned an aide and gave a quick command. When the aide returned, "No, no," said the Shah, "not suitable at all. Henceforth let her be known as Ghozal, for so I command it!" And from that day on to the end of her days she was known only as Ghozal, the beautiful.

The whole time the Shah had gazed at her, Rakhie stood petrified not quite grasping the situation. Not so the rest of the Assyrian contingent, for they knew only too well what the Shah was thinking and were in no frame of mind to linger. As soon as the procession started to move forward they acted quickly. Surrounding young Ghozal, they hurried her home. With the whole community helping, a wedding was soon arranged to the most acceptable suitor. By the time the Shah's men came for her, Ghozal was already a married woman.

The improbable had come to pass. Ghozal's walnut hope chest with all her handstitched bridal trousseau stood against the wall of another room, in another house, under the roof of her new husband. She had not expected marriage for several years. After four years of, however, Ghozal was widowed. Her hasty wedding had been one of convenience to a man much older than she. Since there were no children from that union she was returned into the care of her parents after the customary one-year mourning period. In due course she married my grandfather Qasha (Priest) Mooshi Moorhaj, and they moved to Maragha where he established a small parish.

Maragha, like Urmia, had been an Assyrian settlement and was established several centuries ago on the banks of the noisy, wildly beautiful Sufi Chai River. The Assyrians called their new settlement Mar Agha, loosely translated as "saint sir," which gradually came to sound more like Maragha as it is named today. The Sufi Chai valley with its temperate climate and fertile soil was ideally suited to the needs of the Assyrian settlers. With their love of the land and a strong work ethic they soon had the valley blooming with vines, gardens and orchards.

In the Koh-il-nar hills some three or four miles outside of Maragha, there is an extensive labyrinthine system of caves, named Koheel, that still contain evidence of onetime Assyrian occupation. Some of the caves were enlarged by monks to shelter the settlers in times of jihad. On the rock face of the caves one can still see the water-eroded, scratched outlines of our ancient Syriac script. Outside, on the hillside, are the worn-out remains of a church and monastery. On that same hillside, more than four centuries ago, the Assyrians made their last stand against the might of Islam. After it was all over, the church and monastery were razed to the ground and the hand chiseled rocks and stones were carted away to build other structures in another place. Every effort was made to wipe out all traces of a Christian presence. There was still a small pocket of Assyrians left in the safety of wall-enclosed Maragha until the first two or three years of the twentieth century, but they too had vanished. Then, my grandparents, Mooshi and Ghozal, came to establish a new Assyrian colony. This time around, however, they were shown nothing but kindness and generosity by the community living there. Later, that generosity extended through us to theAssyrian refugees who poured into the city in the aftermath of the mass human destruction of World War I.

Ghozal went to work at her husband's side teaching the women what she had learned at the hospital in Urmia. She taught them the importance of hygiene and good nutrition for building healthy bodies in order to combat the many diseases that plagued them. It was during this period that Ghozal read about a smallpox vaccine being developed in the West. Observing the ravages of  the disease all around her, with great willpower she set out to work on a vaccine of her own. After many months of trial and error she actually developed a vaccine that worked. As a result, there would be no more severely pockmarked faces, blind eyes, or noses partly eaten away, and no more deaths. The constant nagging fear of the disease would be gone forever. Soon Muslim women from surrounding villages came seeking the miracle provided by the Christian "saint" and his wife with their magic "quill." They spread the good news of the vaccine to people in other nearby villages. In time, for further protection against the evil pox, they named their newborn sons Qasha or Qashagha (Priest, or Mr. Priest) after Qasha Mooshi, and their daughters were named Ghozal after the holy man's wife.

Qasha Mooshie and Ghozal had six children. They were Emmanuel, Sanam, John, Sophie, Shushan (my mother), and Arthur. Uncle John became a doctor and career soldier, Lt. Colonel John Tamraz, in the U.S. Armed Forces and personal physician to General Dwight D. Eisenhower and Mamie Eisenhower. During World War II he was the Administrator of American Military Affairs in the Indian-Pacific Front. Ironically, he survived the war only to be killed in a car accident after the war. He was accorded full military honors and lies buried in Arlington Cemetery. In time there would be four more lonely graves, these in our family plot in Tabriz, where the family eventually relocated to. The graves in Tabriz lay desolate and unkempt because there was no one left to care for them. One grave is that of my father, Yoel, another is that of my three-year-old brother, William, who died before I was born. The other two are those of my grandparents, Ghozal and Mooshi.

## An Assyrian Legend

A charming story has been passed down orally in our family for many generations. It is about a distant maternal ancestor and how our Christian family came by its Muslim name of Moorhaj. Around 350 years ago, a gang of marauding Kurds kidnapped a young Assyrian boy from his home near Urmia with the intention of selling him as a harem slave. He must have been an amiable little fellow, for as soon as the Great Khan saw him he instantly adored the boy, took him home, formally adopting him as his own son. We do not know what the little boy's name was as, of course, the Khan would not have kept the boy's original Assyrian name. The Khan renamed him Mirhaj, Mir short for emir, meaning prince, and haj, meaning holy pilgrim.

Mirhaj, thereafter, grew up in the Muslim faith quite unaware of his adoption, or of his Christian heritage. Sometimes, in those long ago times, it happened that great generosity of spirit went hand-in-hand with the savagery. And so it was with the Khan. When Mirhaj was on the threshold of manhood and ready to take up the khanjal against the Christians, the Khan summoned him to his divan and told him the truth about the circumstances of his birth, his kidnapping, and his adoption.

"Now, my son," he said, "it is entirely up to you. You are free to go back and search for your Christian kin, or to stay here as my son and take your place as Khan when I am gone. Think well, my son, and let me know your wish in this matter."

Mirhaj thought long and deeply on the situation and, finally, made the decision to leave his adoptive father and family. He realized that he no longer wanted to take up the sword against the infidel Christians, nor did he want to stay and watch other Kurds bring hell to people whose blood ran in his veins.

The legend does not say whether Mirhaj found his parents, but he did find his paternal uncle, Qasha Oraham, who was the richest man for many miles around. Qasha Oraham and the villagers received Mirhaj with open arms and soon gave his name a more Assyrian sounding tone, Moorhaj. This was to become my mother's maiden name.

Before long, Moorhaj worked his way up in the world and became overseer of his uncle's lands. One day as his men were digging foundations in a field, they struck a large solid object buried deep in the ground. "It is a rock," yelled Moorhaj, thinking fast. "It is too late in the day to try to dig it out now. I will let you go home a little early today, but make sure you are back here bright and early in the morning so we can finish up our work."

When the men had gone Moorhaj started digging excitedly and soon uncovered a large, rusty iron chest full of gold and silver coins. Being a fast worker, as well as a fast thinker, he quickly hid the bulk of the treasure locking the chest securely, and topped it with rubble lodging it firmly back where he had found it.

The next morning when the men returned they were delighted at their find. The master was fetched and rewarded each man handsomely for his diligence and honesty. Naturally, the handsomest reward went to the charming young hero of the story, Moorhaj! Now he was quite rich. In due course he married the master's daughter and became my great, great, great, et cetera, grandfather.

# 21

## Old Fashioned Housekeeping

Our house is always stirring with activity. Grandma, with Mama's consent, runs it smoothly like clockwork. The work in the main living areas is done before we come down in the morning, but the kitchens at the back of the house are full of sound and movement until an hour or so after the main meal of the day, which is served at noon. Then there is a brief lull as everyone rests, given that they have been up and working from six-thirty or seven o'clock in the morning. Work starts again at four o'clock with afternoon tea for the grown-ups and snacks for us children when we come home from school, or from playing. Next, preparation of the evening meal begins and unless guests are expected it is a simple affair. We might have cold meat with a baked potato and various salads, or thick vegetable soup with *bilinchik*, a Russian style meat roll wrapped in thin pastry, and always milk, yogurt, and fresh and dried fruits and nuts.

Everyday after breakfast Grandma has her cart packed with foods such as butter, buttermilk, cheese, perhaps freshly baked bread, and fruit in season from our orchards across the river. She is usually ready to depart and make deliveries to the Assyrian refugees as we prepare to leave for school. I often long to play truant so I can sit next to Grandma and drive the donkey-cart. Better still, I want to sit alone on the driver's seat, all grown up and very beautiful, handling the donkey graciously and accepting the homage of all passersby.

The small dairy where we milk our two household cows is in an adjoining courtyard and always busy. The dairy boys take the cows through the city gates to paddocks on the other side of the river to graze, and bring them back in the evening ready to be milked. Some of the milk is scalded for drinking immediately and the rest is made into yogurt and cheese, or churned into butter. After it is churned, the butter is cut into pats and placed on glossy vine leaves for short-term storage in the icy cold *sard-ab*. Then, fresh and chilled, it is brought upstairs for our daily use. When there is more butter than we immediately need, Grandma cuts it up into small pats to give to Papa's destitute patients.

The sard-ab (also called *ambar* in Assyrian) is a water storage tank and literally means "cold water" in Farsi, the Persian language. It is a large room made of cement-daubed brick and built under the house. Ours is huge to accommodate our extended family. To get to the sard-ab you descend several flights of stairs into the bowels of the earth, or so it seems. Here there is a row of two or three taps connected to a large brick and cement in-ground cistern underneath. The water in the cistern is icy cold. In warm weather, items such as fruit, yogurt, and salad vegetables are immersed in the water for an hour or two to chill before being served.

Water gets delivered to the ambar four times a year through underground channels called *qanats*. The qanat water delivery system is an ancient Persian invention used for either irrigation purposes, or to channel water into towns. Every suburb and every street has its own delivery night. Water sources are privately owned and stay in the same families for generations. The newly delivered water is rather dirty, but it turns sparkling clean after settling on charcoal filter beds. The water transport procedure is manually managed all the way from its source, usually an upland aquifer, to the delivery point. There are qanat openings every few hundred feet snaking their way across the landscape for many miles. Workmen descend into the qanats wading knee-deep in the water to either clean them out, or to plug and unplug the channels to control the direction of flow. They carry bundles of rags as the tools of their trade, using them over and over until they fall to pieces. This sounds horrific by today's standards of cleanliness, but every drop of water in our house is filtered and boiled before being used. We children are repeatedly warned never, never to drink water straight from the tap. Other households do not neccesarily take these precautions and, as a result, typhoid fever is endemic. There is hardly a family in the community that has not lost one or more children to this disease, or to diphtheria and tuberculosis.

Whatever we need at home always seems to be available; from homemade bread to homemade candles, to knitted mittens, socks and stockings, to jellies, jams, preserves, pickles, sun-dried tomatoes and dried vegetables by the bushel for the long winter ahead, they are all stored in large quantities. We children don't quite understand how much planning and effort it takes to make all this abundance possible.

Grandma cards new wool, spins it at her spinning wheel, and knits it into garments. Once a year she has all our quilts emptied of their wool filling, and has the wool and covers washed separately. The wool is dried, combed, and teased until it is clean and fluffy againt, hen it is stuffed back into clean quilt covers. The quilt always has a top sheet pinned into place with large safety pins to keep it clean. Top sheets are longer than bottom sheets, covering the *doona* (approximately like a duvet) and nearly encasing it.

Laundry, including bedsheets, is done once a week by hand. It is a labor-intensive job that takes all day to complete. Two washerwomen come every Monday at seven a.m. and work well into the early evening hours before they are done. Inside, three or four charcoal irons are constantly kept hot to tackle the dry laundry that comes off the clotheslines. Sometimes the person doing the ironing starts to look pale and languid and to complain of *oogar*, the Russian term for headache from charcoal fumes. She reclines on a sofa and enjoys becoming the center of attention, and the respite she gets from work. Another woman has to take her place at the ironing board in order to complete the job in a timely manner. Mama brings cold drinks and makes sure there is proper ventilation and that irons are not brought inside while still smoking. When wash day is over the house feels fresh and spotless, and everyone breathes a sigh of relief to have it end.

In the autumn we store fresh fruit for the winter in our cold, subterranean cellar. Apples and pears are packed in sawdust, while cantaloupes and watermelons are arranged on hessian mats on the cold cellar floor. As mentioned before, grape milagh is hung from the cellar ceiling, row after row, like soldiers on the march. Partially dried nectarines are stuffed with sugared almond meal and left to dry again. Dried fruits are stored with fruit leathers (made from the mash of boiled down fruit) and nut concoctions in wooden chests set against the cool cellar walls. We also have storage chests filled with walnuts,hazelnuts, *sultanas* (yellow raisins), and dark raisins, which are brought weekly from the orchards to be shelled or rubbed in towels to clean off bits of stalk, sand, or other debris. All the fruits and nuts came from our own orchards, processed by our own staff, managed by my own amazing grandmother. These same procedures have probably gone on for countless hundreds of years before I was even born.

And now for the staff of life. Bread, called *lavash*, is baked in huge quantities in the month of October, when we still have plenty of sunshine to dry the parchment thin sheets, and is stored for the winter. Our bakehouse, or *tanoor-khana*, is a large outbuilding where we store everything needed for baking bread and making pasta. The women who bake the bread are experts, professionals, and their services must be booked well in advance. A good house mistress knows how many days she needs to book in a particular year and chooses the month and day to suit her entertainment schedule. Bakers arrive the evening before baking day in order to prepare the dough, and build the fire in the cylindrical in-ground oven. They must use a slow burning, low flaming wood that they will stoke several times in the night when they get up to knead the dough. After a night of building and stoking the fire, layers of smouldering hot coals form in the bottom of the cylinder creating hours of baking heat in the tanoor, or oven.

During the night the bakers have divided the dough into large balls, punched them in the middle and left them to rise again. One woman, sits cross-legged at a low, round table, rolls one of the balls of dough into a twelve to fourteen inch circle, then with a quick movement flings it onto the floured arms of a second woman who elongates the mass a little as she catches it. Now the second woman flips the oval shaped mass from arm to arm, elongating it further to about three feet long by twelve to twenty inches wide. Next she tosses it to the baker, the head woman, who catches the sheet in the middle and with one deft movement drapes it onto a yard long, straw filled, convex form. The form has a strap at the back to fit her hand. With another quick movement she puts her hand into the strap, and bending over, she slaps the bread dough onto the hot sides of the hot tanoor. It probably takes no more than one minute for the dough to complete its travels from the first woman to the oven. These master bakers could probably perform these procedures in their sleep, they have done it so many times.

At any given moment, there are three or four sheets of bread plastered against the sides of the oven in different stages of baking. When the bread starts to peel away from the oven wall it is ready to come out. The baker pulls out the lavash using a very long fork and a spatula-like utensil and flings it onto canvas sheets to cool and dry out in the sun. Later, stacks of the bread will be taken to the cellars where they will be placed on a special breadstand that is hollow in the center for ventilation. The bread is stacked in overlapping sheets around and around the stand, perhaps three feet high, then covered by another long, heavy sheet. It will keep perfectly there for months.

Tanoors like ours have been a tradition in the Middle East since the days of Abraham. Nowadays, the oven cylinders are made of pre-cast, hardened cement and sunk into the floor of the tanoor-khana. Ours is a massive eight feet deep and about three-and-a-half feet across. Cleaning out the ashes is another demanding job. One man climbs in and hands buckets of ash to another man who kneels at the top edge. When this chore is completed both men are ashen faced and grey haired.

By sunrise when the baking has gotten into full swing we awake to the luscious aroma that drifts into our bedrooms from the tanoor-khana. We flock barefoot across the courtyard rubbing the sleep from our eyes, as if mesmerized, and lured by the savory smell of the freshly baked bread. We love to sit cross-legged around the tanoor and sample the fresh, hot, and crisp bread spread generously with butter and cottage cheese, already prepared for our breakfast. Later, the stored bread can be eaten dry and crunchy, but usually we dampen it with water and leave it covered with a clean cloth and allow it to soften. Then we can spread it with butter, cottage cheese, chopped lettuce, spring onions, or whatever we like, and roll it up like a wrap.

Clarified butter is processed in the bakehouse for long-term winter storage. If we can't produce enough of our own, Mr. Gregorian buys more from small subsistence farmers in the surrounding villages. Sometimes Papa's Turkish or Kurdish patients pay for his medical services with goatskins filled with butter. Raw butter from the villages is not very clean so it must be heated in a large cauldron over a low flame, and brought to a slow simmer. After it melts, the butter is carefully skimmed of every bubble and bit of scum, which consists mostly of milk solids or other debris. This job requires patient and skillful handling so as not to burn the butter and spoil the taste. Depending on the quantity, this process could take up to five or six hours. After it cools the pure butterfat is carefully poured into a large, clay Aladdin jar big enough to hold one of Ali Baba's forty thieves, and carted down to the cellars for storage. All such storage jars are positioned on one of several large stands sitting on frames that stretch along the cellar walls, hanging by their fat middles a few inches off the ground.

By the time we arrive home from school later in the day, the liquid butter is ready for pouring into jars. We run straight to the tanoor-khana where we know that treats await us; sheets of crunchy lavash, cottage cheese, butter, fruit, and scalded milk. We crush some lavash into small bowls of liquid butter making a rich and delicious mash. Our employees eat theirs with their fingers, skillfully using the thumb, index, and middle fingers to roll the mixture into tidy balls. They do a better job of cleaning their bowls than we do with our civilized utensils. Although we are strongly discouraged to do so, we try their method of eating, but fail miserably, so we are quite happy to stick to our conventional knives, forks, and spoons!

The tanoor-khana serves another important role; it is the meeting place for the household staff. The maids, the two dairy women, Sultan's groom, Papa's attendant, Aram, and others gather there to have their bit of gossip and drink a glass of sweet black *chai* (tea) before going off again to different parts of the house to their various duties. Here, too, when all is quiet, Pari Baji and her gateman hold their trysts, perennially whispering their awesome secret into one another's ears.

With the passage of time, though modern ways of life were creeping in, Mama continued to keep a large house in Tabriz, maintaining the old, gracious lifestyle until the end of World War II. Aladdin jars still stood row upon row around the basement walls, grape milagh hung from the ceilings, and wooden boxes on the floor still held all the delectable dried fruit and nut concoctions. Once a week, a truck would arrive from Maragha, forty miles to the south, bringing us large baskets filled with fruit and vegetables from our family orchards. As always, some we would eat fresh, some we stored, and some we would give to friends and neighbors. Though we had moved from Maragha to Tabriz, and a few modern amenities had arrived, life went on as usual. But, our dear Papa and Grandma were no longer with us.

After World War II, things seemed to stay the same for a while. Then suddenly, it all changed. Our province of Azerbaijan seceded from Iran and joined the communist Soviet Republic of Azerbaijan, across the River Aras. Property prices plummeted as people fled the city in panic. Mama was pestered daily by settlers from the Russian side demanding to rent rooms, considering her home communal property. When she refused, telling them that this was a private home, they threatened to inform the *Comintern* (a communist organization formed by Lenin in 1919) that one person occupied a dwelling large enough to house several families. We were anxious for Mama's safety so we sold everything and moved out of the new Soviet zone.

The new republic did not last long and the former Iranian Azerbaijan returned to Iran with the aid of negotiations between the Allies. Eventually, businesses began returning to Tabriz and property prices sky-rocketed. For us, though, it was too late. The shocking changes had all taken place too suddenly and once we had left our home and old lifestyle, we knew we could never go back.

ﻡﻡﻡ

# 22

# An Old Fashioned Wedding: The Sign of the Seventh Day

We have been invited to an Armenian wedding and, now that I am nearly eight years old, I will be allowed to go to see the bride in all her ceremonial finery. Mama says that this could very well be one of the last large old-fashioned weddings, as the Christian community has gradually been influenced by Western style practices. Inviting the whole family, almost the whole community, is customary and expected in thee traditional weddings. The most formal invitations are made by word-of-mouth from the mother of the bride, these being granted to only the most honored guests.

A traditional wedding was celebrated over a period of seven days and nights, each day having a special name and ceremony associated with it. The first five days were: The Day of the Gift Bearing, The Day of Applying the Henna, The Day of Showing of the Trousseau, The Day of the Hammam, and The Day of the Bridegroom's Visit. The sixth day was The Day of the Wedding Ceremony. Finally, the Seventh Day (as I learned later from a book I wasn't supposed to read) was when the bride's mother self-conciously whispered the secret of married life into her daughter's blushing ears. Until then I had been quite content to remain a child innocently playing in the sun, but suddenly I was eager to grow up quickly and have the secret whispered into my blushing ear! But, the Seventh Day shall remain undisclosed for now - for you would never believe it!

Engagements were usually short, almost as binding as the marriage itself, and celebrated ceremonially by a priest. The bride-to-be wore a gold wedding band from that day on and it was only after her marriage that she was given jewelery other than gold. Any contact between the engaged couple was arranged by the family and was strictly chaperoned. When the future groom came calling on his fiance her mother remained close by. She knitted, furiously clicking her knitting needles and watched from the corner of one eye, while he tried to unobtrusively hold the girl's hand, coaxing her to say that she loved him more than anything else in the world. She blushed shyly while he worshipped her, putting her on a pedestal pure and chaste as an angel, to be his very own one day.

Five of the six wedding days followed ancient rituals called the Book and Candle; the book being the Bible and its injunctions, and the candle symbolizing the illumination of their path through life for the newly married couple. By the end of each ceremony and the festivities that followed the priest was, more often than not, a little tipsy after imbibing too much ceremonial wine. The men would drink a little wine, but the women were all teetotalers who drank only tea and sharbat. On The Day of Showing the Trousseau, all wedding gifts were displayed and the bride's hope chest was opened. A woman well versed in these matters lifted out each item and spread it out for display calling attention to the fact that everything was hand-stitched and embroidered by the fair hands of the bride-to-be herself; bed linens, tablecloths, bath and kitchen towels, personal items such as bras, petticoats, everything. There were also several hand-stitched shirts for her husband-to-be, her father-in-law, and many other pieces.

On The Day of the Hammam, the bride's eyebrows were plucked into a thin arched line for the first time in her life, and her facial and body hair was removed. This was done skillfully by a professional woman who regularly provided married women with these services. She used a set of double strings that were wound up so tightly together that they became elastic as the two ends were pulled apart from each other. A mesmerizing rhythm and hum was created with the stretching and retraction of the strings. As she pulled the string set in and out between her hands she applied them to the skin causing the hairs to get trapped between the threads and be pulled out by the roots. All this time the poor girl was never left alone having a dozen or more women always around her. The worst was yet to come, however. On The Day of the Hammam, or public bath, she was escorted to the bath-house with great ceremony accompanied by drums and *ashogh* (a guitar-like instrument), and female relatives and friends who openly rejoiced that they could now avenge themselves for their own past suffering! The bride-to-be was scrubbed and groomed practically out of her skin by a dozen or more hands, then drummed back home again to a waiting crowd of other women and girls. The festivities continued with tea, music, dancing, and teasing. By this time the girl must have felt really sick, wishing she had never been born, and that all men had been transported far beyond the North Sea. Better still, that all her tormentors had been transported somewhere beyond recall, and she and her love left alone to wed quietly and be together at last. Alas, there was still the ordeal of the Seventh Day to face, and the forty days beyond!

Men had no role to play at the bride's house. Close male relatives and a few honored male guests came on certain evenings to a separate part of the house, to drink tea and play backgammon, smiling all the while at the sounds of their women's revelry.

At the women's party, when a solo dancer was especially good, or beautiful, or popular, the noise grew louder, the music faster, and the crowd clapped and yelled, "Shah-bash, shah-bash" (literally meaning "be king"), which was to say, rise as high as a king and prosper. Then money, usually in small denomination coins, but sometimes gold and silver, came showering down at the dancer's feet. The money was used to pay for the musicians, or to help defray wedding expenses. The dancer then bowed to someone else in the crowd, calling her out to the floor to join her. After another round of dancing, the first dancer retreated gracefully, leaving the other one to carry on. I was dying to be asked and, at last, my turn came. Everyone started to shout, "Shamir's Dance, Shamir's Dance," which was my particular specialty. When Papa heard that I was dancing he came in with some of the other men laughing and clapping as, on my haunches, I did fast Russian-style footwork to the music, not easy I might add, and stood up to do more wild Ruski-style prancing around the room. All the while, I looked for someone to bow to. That is when I spotted bashful Mama trying to make herself as inconspicuous as possible. When I bowed to her the cheering grew louder, and the Shah Bashes became deafening. Papa got carried away while being urged on by the other men and showered us with coins.

At last, the sixth day, The Day of the Wedding Ceremony, had arrived. The wedding ceremony was usually held in the evening at lamp lighting time. As evening approached the bride was dressed and her makeup applied by her attendants. This would be the first time in her life she had worn makeup, and it might be the last, as it was not customary nor proper for women to paint their faces. The make-up was chalk white to symbolize purity and would be wiped off at the appropriate time.

Suspense was building in the streets as everyone stood waiting for the bridal party to arrive. The musicians were waiting for a cue from the bride's brothers who were on the look-out for the bride and her attendants. Now one of them was shouting, "They are coming, they are almost here." This was the moment everyone had been waiting for. The groom's party, complete with its own musicians, approached the bridal party to join together and proceed to the church.

They would walk by torchlight displaying the bride and her trousseau and wedding gifts to the spectators lining the streets. The gifts and trousseau were placed on five-foot-long trays and carried atop the heads of specially hired men. People either joined in the procession, or positioned themselves on the sidelines to view the bride and her trousseau of samovars, china, lamps, and household ornaments all being carried on the huge oblong trays.

The Armenian Orthodox church, which had no pews, was already almost filled to capacity by uninvited guests when the wedding procession arrived. A path had to be cleared to allow the bride and groom to get to the main altar. All members of the two families were there, with the notable exception of the bride's mother who, as a rule, does not atttend the church ceremon. She cannot relax, or rejoice, until the Seventh Day. On that day it will be determined whether she may receive an accolade, the highest praise from her husband and the community, or she may hang her head in shame as an unworthy wife and unfit mother.

The mother may hardly sleep that night, tossing and turning, wondering if she has brought up her daughter properly, has she done all that she can, has she been vigilant enough? She suffers through the night and rises at dawn preparing herself to face the ordeal of The Seventh Day. She busies herself around her house, short-tempered, snappy, pricking her ears to every sound on the street, waiting . . . the endless waiting. Then, pale as moonlight, she clutches her breast and drops into a chair, having ordered her other children out of the room. In time, the awaited guest arrives. An elderly woman is ushered in carrying a parcel wrapped in a snow-white, lacy cloth called the *bukhcha*. With great drama, the old woman slowly unfolds the bukhcha from each corner. "Will this unwrapping never end," thinks the mother? Lifting a white bedsheet out of its wrapping, the old woman holds it up for all to see the bright red stain, the victorious sign of The Seventh Day!

# 23

## Muharram and Ashura

*"I am bidden to surrender myself to the Lord of the Worlds. He it is who created us out of the dust."*

The Koran, Sura 40

There is a strange stillness in the air, a quiet restraint that makes people want to speak in subdued voices and walk on tiptoes. In the streets and bazaars business goes on as usual though this, too, seems to suffer from a weighty malaise. All activities have been subdued. There are no weddings, no parties, and all laughter and joy is suspended. This is Muharram, the Shiite month of mourning, the commemoration of the martyrdom by decapitation in battle of the Prophet Hussein in 680 A.D. The Muslim year was 58 A.H., After Hejira, or the Prophet Mohammad's flight from Mecca to Medina.

The Iranian and Arabic year is a lunar one that is shorter than the solar year so every few years a month is added to bring it in alingment with the astronomical, or solar, year. Because of this, Muharram is not on a fixed date, but moves across the seasons. I have seen the rites performed in the height of summer with the drowsy humming of bees in the sunshine, and in the depth of winter with snow piled high on the ground and the breath an opaque mist in the air. Winter or summer, rain or snow, storm or lightning, the processions and the enactment of the tragedy go on day after day. They build to the climax, the unfolding of the complete tragic drama on the final day of the Passion Play, the Ashura. No matter how dramatic the events leading up to the Ashura, one is never prepared for the stupendous, incredible finale, the awesome final performance.

The story began in the early years of Islam when the Prophet Mohammed died and his father-in-law, Abu Bakr, was elected *caliph*, or successor. The succession of caliphs that descended from his lineage were to become the Sunni sect. The name Sunni derives from the Arabic word *sunnah*, meaning the words and actions, or example, of the Prophet. However, a breakaway faction formed, which believed the succession should continue through the Prophet's daughter Fatima and her husband Ali, who was also the Prophet's cousin. This group came to be known as Shiites, derived from shortening the term *Shiat Ali*, or partisans of Ali.

In 58 A.H. a battle between the two factions took place in the desert of Karbala (located in modern day Iraq.) The breakaway party was led by the Prophet's younger son Hussein who made a claim for the caliphate to honor his father's lineage. Hassan, Ali's elder son, had given up his claim to the caliphate, but had been poisoned to death anyway. Hussein's army was much smaller, which made the odds against them great from the outset. The contest was ultimately lost, with Hussein getting decapitated in the fierce heat of battle.

Imam Hussein's death is commemorated each year by Shiite Muslims in the month of Muharram with a re-enactment of the events of 58 A.H. Throughout the month, leading up to the Ashura, groups of male mourners dress in black clothing, their heads shaved and black-kerchiefed, with ash rubbed faces, pour out of mosques and run through the streets beating their breasts, and chant mournful condolences with regard to Hussein's death in Karbala. They do not stop until they reach the next mosque. Every mosque participates, competing with the others by way of the discipline, presentation, and performance of its members. Arriving at their destination, the mourners impart their message of death and destruction in battle. They exhibit their commiseration as if the events had just happened and they are the only surviving witnesses. Many are taken ill with emotion and exhaustion, and some become so frenzied as to need restraint from further participation. Deaths have been known to occur but, as in Christian martyrdom, they are accordingly assured of a place in Paradise. The remaining mourners, their numbers now increased by men waiting on the sidelines, go on to the next mosque, and the next, until the circuit is completed and they return to the original starting point. Here they disband, slake their thirst with glasses of sharbat, and have their cuts and bruises treated. Then it is back to their shops and places of business, until their turn comes again to be immersed in this pageantry of grief.

Some of the groups are flagellants baring their torsos summer or winter, beating themselves with chains until their bodies are raw with wounds and bleeding profusely. Others pierce their bodies with hooked nails hanging weights such as large metal locks and other heavy objects from the nails to cause more pain and injury, thus replicating the wounds of their saints in battle.

In the first few days of Muharram I awaken in the night to the clamor of the hourly processions. The sounds of loud, mournful chanting seem to hang in the still air long after the marchers are swallowed up by the gloomy night. By contrast, the deep silence between processions induces a heavy, suffocating feeling. After a while I get used to it and no longer run to the window every time I hear a group of mourners approaching. While we sleep in relative comfort, wakeful vigils are being kept in every Muslim home. Muslim women participate alongside their men by tending to all their needs. The men will need comforting and preparation for the ordeals of the forthcoming days that will leave them emotionally and physically exhausted. *Hammans*, public baths, are also open all night for the weary to take steam baths and showers. And basement *gymkhanas*, men's fitness clubs, stay open offering massage and therapeutic exercise for tired or injured limbs.

There are strange goings on in our stables. Papa's proud and beautiful Arabian stallion, Sultan, is on a special diet to make him more docile and add sheen to his fur. He is groomed daily, almost hourly, making his mane and tail silky. His hooves are trimmed and polished to a perfect shine. Mourners come to his stall daily and talk to him gently, kiss him, and whisper sweetly like a lover into the beloved's ear. As he gets more accustomed to all the attention, mourners are allowed to come running in and embrace him while commiserating with him on the death of his master,

Hussein. To them, at this moment he is Zuljina, the dead Imam's horse. On The Day, the Ashura, Sultan will also march in the parade as the Imam's beloved horse.

The intensity of the mourning gradually builds up to a peak during the month and now, at last, the day is here, the Ashura, the day of the passion play. We are tucked into our beds at the usual hour and Mama reads to us girls while Papa is with the boys.

"Good night, Mama, good night, Papa," we yell after the tenth hug and kiss. "Promise to wake us up early in time to watch the Ashura."

"Yes, yes, we promise, but go to sleep now or you will never wake up in time."

## Ashura

By the next morning the procession is already underway. The Imam Hussein, his followers, soldiers, slaves, women and children, and all their belongings are moving out of Medina to meet their fate. The cavalry proceeds on magnificent horses, the infantry in ancient costume, then come the slaves carrying large oblong trays on their heads loaded with showy lamps and vases, beautiful ornaments, small priceless rugs, embroidered silk clothing, and the like, all borrowed from wealthy families just for today, because everyone wants to participate in some way. Then come the mules carrying in their panniers food, utensils, and china, all the trappings of a large household on the move. The more humble neighborhoods that cannot put on a showy display are aided by well-to-do Christians families who contribute valuable items to the local mosque for the procession. This offer of sympathetic support is a much appreciated gesture creating an alliance of goodwill between Muslims and Christians, though a formal one.

The procession's cheerful mood abruptly shifts as if an unexpected tragedy has just taken place. A group of black clad, ashen faced mourners arrives, beating their chests, chanting that a battle has been fought and lost, and that Imam Hussein has been martyred. The rest of the Muslim crowd joins in the lamentations as Sultan appears, looking proud and beautiful, draped with a rich silk rug and the bloodied, "headless" body of Hussein sitting on top. A model of his decapitated head is carried separately on a small bloodstained tray. Groups of black clad mourners come running toward Sultan and fling their arms around his neck, kiss him, cry over him and, chant sorrowfully, consoling with him on his master's death. As the crowd wails we children also become tearful at the sight of so much grief, even though we have been told that it is only a re-enactment of something that happened many centuries ago. Mama tries not to watch, taking only the occasional peek. When the main event approaches, she withdraws to the back of the roof, covering her ears with her hands declaring that she is no Roman and does not have the stomach for it. She is only here to keep an eye on us children. On this occasion she cannot trust Pari Baji or Martha to watch us attentively.

The procession continues for some time after Sultan has gone. But now, the crowd is getting restless, whispering, craning necks, looking toward the top of the street. They are anxiously awaiting the last stage of the show, the grand finale. In different mosques all over town, separate groups of men are being prepared in the courtyards for the final stage. These are volunteers, mendicants seeking the grace and favor of Allah, who have made special vows and prayers and who during the month have prepared themselves spiritually for the martyrdom to which they may be called on this day. Death is a distinct possibility for which they are ready, for on this special day death means waking up in Paradise with its promised rewards.

Over their black clothes the men wear ankle length white shirts, which are short sleeved and free flowing. Their heads and faces are clean shaven. Each man carries a wide bladed sword and beats his head with the flat side of the blade to the rhythm of the chanting, and repetitively calls on the name of their dead leader Hussein and his brother Hassan. The chanting gradually escalates to a crescendo, the swords rise in the air and plunge sharp edge down slashing and lacerating their numb heads. Blood spurts from the wounds staining face and hands and snow-white garments. The bloodied men become unrecognizable with the stains of battle. They form into a long chain holding the sword in their right hand, while the left hand lightly holds his neighbor's shoulder. The man at the head of the line leads the long chain of his bloodstained comrades, thirty, forty, fifty, or more, into the street following the procession's route. They walk sideways along the narrow streets, their backs to the wall, and moving slowly, swords held up, as they continue to call out the names of the Prophet's grandsons.

Emotions are fully charged and at times get out of control. As tension builds up, suddenly one man, and then another throws his sword high into the air, at which time it falls awkwardly, slashing his already badly lacerated head. Some men faint from the pain, or the shock of the blows, and are taken away. The human chain must re-form so as to continue to the main mosque, the Masjedeh Juma. My father is the only Christian I know of who has witnessed the climax of the Ashura inside a Masjedeh Juma. A few men die, some are very sick, and all are physically and emotionally exhausted, but spiritually, they feel rewarded and happy.

I have watched the passion play of Muharram many times in several cities over the years. It is always the same, the only differences being in the size, the richness, and the variety in the presentations. The impact, especially the main event or the finale, is always the same, never less than stunning. The last time I saw Sultan play the role of Zuljina was in the Ashura of 1923. I do not know what happenned after that as we moved to Tabriz without him. Being the magnificent creature he was, I have no doubt that he went on to perform that role for the entire prime years of his life.

# 24

# The Straw Hat

Papa and Homer are due back from Tabriz this afternoon. We missed them very much since they left last week. But we know that Papa never comes home empty handed, so we are eagerly awaiting their return. Papa is always loaded with gifts for all of us, and this time Homer enclosed a little note for me in Papa's letter saying that he would be bringing me something nice as well. The excitement is almost too much to bear and the hands of the wall clock, which we check every few minutes, give the impression of being stuck. Mama also seems impatient. She often checks her gold-leaf watch that hangs on a long, thick gold chain, which is wound twice around her neck and pinned to her breast like a brooch.

Now that the time has come for us to make the move to Tabriz, Papa has been looking for a centrally located house that is large enough to accomodate our household and his clinic. He writes that every moment he can spare from other business he spends at the American Hospital reacquainting himself with the smells and sounds of a large medical institution. He is happy that, at last, he will be in a position to accept a long-standing offer to join the hospital staff in Tabriz.

Angel still lisps while asking, "When are Papa and Homer coming home?" The two little ones are really beautiful and Mama always dresses them like twins. At the moment they are wearing pretty pink, flounced dresses with hems set fashionably below mid-calf, white cotton stockings held up with garters, and wide pink butterfly ribbons in their hair. Willie is busily trotting back and forth to the street gates to make sure that our gateman is there to let us out when we go to meet Papa and Homer.

We know exactly when they will arrive, about twenty to thirty minutes before the caravans are due to avoid the commotion, dust, and smell of camels. In turn, the caravans arrive an hour before sunset to leave time for the street cleaners to sweep and water down the dust before the call to evening prayer. Traveling is done only by daylight to avoid dangerous bandits on the dark roads of night. Posting houses are conveniently situated a comfortable day's journey apart for camel caravans, horse drawn carriages, or coaches. Small tea-houses are scattered here and there between the posting houses, all of them lice and flea ridden, places where you do not want to linger any longer than absolutely necessary. Whenever anyone comes home from a journey Mama makes them go straight to the bathhouse and take off every stitch of clothing to be thoroughly washed.

When family or friends travel it is customary to make a short journey of one or two hours to see them off, and the same distance to meet them on their return. At long last, the time has come for us to go meet our returning travelers. We are only going as far as the river banks today, because Papa and Homer have been away for just a short time. At the city gate an officer acknowledges Mama by saluting her.

"Salam aleikum, Khanum. It will be nice to see the doctor again. We have missed him on his daily trips in and out of the city. And Sultan too. Mashallah, what a magnificent horse. Go with God, Khanum."

We cross the humped bridge and wait impatiently, each one eager to be the first to spot Papa's carriage. I see it as it comes into view over the hill. It raises billows of dust as it courses down the winding road. We lose sight of it in the foliage of the surrounding orchards, then it comes into view again, nearer and nearer after each curve. Now it disappears again around another bend in the road, moving agonizingly slowly. Oh to see Papa and Homer again, and all those lovely presents! As the carriage rounds the last bend we all run, pushing and shoving to get closer. We climb all over Papa and Homer, hugging, and kissing them enthusiastically. Soon we are yelling and asking Papa for our presents.

"Give a poor man a chance, will you?" says Papa laughing as he hugs Mama. "Let's go home first."

"No, no. Now, now," we yell in unison.

Knowing us only too well, Papa, with Homer's help, has already unpacked our presents and laid them out on the spare seat of the carriage. One item I notice stands out vividly. It is a straw hat with a shiny pink ribbon hanging down the back. Surely this is the most beautiful hat in the world. For a few days that hat becomes my most prized possession. I put it on my head when Papa hands it to me, and there it stays all afternoon and into the evening. No amount of persuasion, or reasoning, will make me take it off, especially after I nearly lost it. The hat would have stayed on my head all night had someone not removed it while I slept. I was so afraid of crushing it that I slept sitting up in bed, leaning against several pillows.

I was lucky to keep that hat in my possession at all. Almost as soon as it was unpacked and on my head, it met with an accident. We were still talking and laughing and climbing in and out of the carriage when one of our young stable boys came along with our one and only donkey. The little donkey was used to pulling the produce cart to and from the orchards. We had other horses and ponies, but we loved that particular donkey with a passion that is hard to explain. We all wanted to ride him home instead of riding with our parents in the carriage. We could not be persuaded otherwise. So Homer, Willie, and I were loaded onto the donkey's back and into the river to ford across. The river at this point is shallow, fed by irrigation channels upstream. It is very pretty and crystal clear. The water murmurs and gurgles peacefully over the clean washed, colorful stones that sparkle in the filtered sunshine. We were laughing and urging the donkey to go faster when suddenly the saddle started to shift dumping all three of us into the river. Papa, the stable boy, and others were soon knee deep in water trying to help us up, but I would have none of it. Wet and bedraggled, I broke away and raced after my hat, howling as I watched my beautiful present sail gracefully away toward the cataract under the bridge. Some kind person downstream managed to retrieve my hat and, though dripping wet, it was soon back on my head where it stayed as an almost permanent fixture for several days.

At home I asked Homer for the present he had promised to bring me from Tabriz. "Oh yes," he said very casually, searching his pockets for my special treat. Out came a couple of knuckle bones, some keys that opened no doors or treasure chests that I know of, a forbidden homemade slingshot with a few stones, and whatever other odd things boys carry in their pockets. And finally, "Here it is," he said as he handed me a piece of stringy, fluff covered meat saved from last evening's meal at a posting house. My stomach turned, but knowing well the bottomless pit that Homer called his stomach, and how much restraint it must have taken him to save the meat for me, I accepted it with a show of gratitude. Then immediately, and very graciously, I offered it my siblings. Agnes and Angel turned up their little noses in disgust, but Willie, possessing a similar pit to Homer's, had no such reservations and ate the thing with relish.

# 25

# The Lone Wolf and the Coral Snake

It is May 1923, spring has arrived bringing sunshine and fragrant blossoms once again. We love playing outside during the sunny hours of the day and in the cold nights, comfortably settled in our beds, we talk and dream about summer vacation and the long warm months ahead. But now we have to work and study hard to pass our exams, for the stakes are high. We can be held back one, two, or even three years if we do not perform to class standards.

Every year, a day or two after our promotion certificates are handed out and the summer holidays officially begin, we move up to our summer house. It is situated on the mountain high above the malarial valley that Maragha is. And every year, with monotonous regularity, when the summer house is checked over after the heavy snows have melted, it is found to be missing all of the verandah timbers that run around the top level, and all the doors and windows. Anything that will burn has been carted away to be used for firewood by the few mountain locals who remain there year-round. Only a few very poor Muslim families live on the mountain. They are fairly safe from marauding bandits because they have nothing much to lose. Still, Papa would much rather replace the verandahs every year than leave a family without enough firewood to keep warm in their state of snowed-in isolation, listening to the mournful howling of wolves all winter.

Every spring before we move in, the verandahs, doors, and windows must be replaced and the household furniture moved up by donkey-cart. Not only furniture, but furnishings such as bedding, kitchen cupboards, and utensils. In the same way, everything that can move, or be removed, goes down with us by cart in the autumn and stored in the basement for next summer.

It is Sunday and Mr. Gregorian has come over after church to remind Mama and Papa that it is time to go up the mountain to inspect the summer house. On his way out he stops for a minute to kick a ball around with us and asks if we would like to go up with him. We yell, "Yes please! Yes please!" and run inside helter-skelter to ask our parents if we will be allowed to go. As we come into the parlor I stand still at the door for a few seconds with my eyes glued to the beautiful, handmade silk rug hanging on the opposite wall, the rug that will one day pay for Bobby's education in the United States. Pinned diagonally across the rug, undulating in sinuous curves just as in real life, is the transparent shed skin of a snake, fully six feet long. We think it is the skin of "THE" coral snake - not any old coral snake, but "THE" coral snake.

Persia, like all ancient lands, has its folklore tales of princes and princesses turned by witchcraft into frogs or dogs, and of snake kings and queens that speak with human voices and wear jeweled crowns; snakes who have power beyond our imagination and can grant your heart's desire if you have rendered their species a special service, or bring you bad luck if you have harmed them in any way. Being children, we believe wholeheartedly in fairy tales and bejeweled snakes, but personally, I have never seen anything less kingly, or queenly, than the snakes on the mountains of Maragha. They are miserable looking creatures, short, skinny and dark, not aggressive. At times, they even behave as if they are blind as well as deaf as they slither by, ignoring us completely.

So what is a six-foot coral snake (not even a native of northwestern Persia) doing in the mountains of Maragha? No one knows. We only know that his den is somewhere near our summer house and that, if one can believe it, he has lived there for as long as the oldest man can remember. Although he has been seen as far as one or two miles away, he has always returned to his underground "palace" near our house.

When Papa bought that property, shortly after I was born, he was warned by the previous owner, "Doctor Khan, don't ever hurt that snake. He is the heart and soul of this property and the protector of the hearth. If you leave him alone he will protect you and bless your house. If you try to harm him, he will bring you bad luck and you will die."

Of course, Papa laughed at the absurdity of the superstition. He did not believe in snakes with magic powers, nor in the existence of a huge coral snake loose in the mountains of Maragha, so far away from its natural habitat. That is, not until he caught a brief glimpse of the snake when the foundation of the house was being dug. Its red and golden yellow rings were shimmering through the green foliage in the brilliant sunshine. He only glimpsed about three feet of the creature's tail - enough to convince him that part of the legend, at least, was true. I cannot remember all the colors of that snake's skin, but the memory of coral rings is still vivid in my mind. I recall that he was very beautiful, and could well believe that he wore a jeweled crown while holding court in his underground palace, ruling over all the creatures of the land.

En route to the mountain we enjoy the ride in Mr. Gregorian's cart. The drive is scenic, the sunshine brilliant, and the exhilarating smells and sounds of spring are everywhere. As we go over the humped bridge we hang on for dear life so as not to slide backward and fall out of the cart. The river is running wild with the spring thaw, roaring mightily, its waters so turgid and murky that you can no longer see the colorful, clean-washed stones at the bottom. We certainly do not feel like wading in it now.

As soon as we cross the bridge Homer, Willie, and I jump out of the cart and run up the winding road to show Mr. Gregorian that we still remember the way to the house. Around the last turn, and facing us at the end of a 150 foot long *varazan*, is our two story summerhouse. It gapes blindly at us, just as we knew it would, minus verandah posts, doors, and windows. Because of the damage done to it every winter, the house is built of the cheapest material, adobe. This is not only because bricks, as well as any wooden fixtures, would be torn out and carted away, but also because we have all kinds of undesirable, unlawful tenants who are trapped there after the raging winter blizzards that keep them from coming back down the mountain.

The house and varazan occupy a long, wide, slightly curved natural fold of the mountainside. It is ideal for our lifestyle, an almost self-sufficient household. The varazan is an adobe covered section of ground on which summer fruits are dried in the fall. In the summer the flat roof of the house is used for drying and the varazan is our playground. When we go back down to the city in September the roof, balconies and the varazan are put into service for fruit drying.

The plan of the house is simple. It faces north and south: North for coolness and shade, and south for sunshine. For safety reasons (from bandits and snakes) and better views of the valley below, the living quarters are on the second level, while the kitchen and all other service areas are downstairs. The living areas open out to the verandahs on both sides. The south view looks across the varazan to where we are now standing at the foot of a clump of trees, and to the winding path that leads down to the Sufi Chai and Maragha. At the back it looks down a slight slope, which is cultivated in grapevines and fruit trees, to a stream that is a tributary of the Sufi Chai, dividing our property into two. At the far side of the thirty foot wide stream is a thicket of tall timber, the dark abode of the dreaded Desha-Bakhtati. We dare not venture any closer to it than a few feet away, for it is here that on full moon nights they dance their wild dances under the towering trees, shrieking so horribly that anyone hearing them is immediately turned into stone!

The grapevines on the north slope are supported on long rows of five-foot-high pyramidal mounds of piled earth that run east to west for maximum exposure to sunshine. The pyramids stand between twenty to thirty feet long, depending on the lay of the land, and are clustered in blocks of ten or more rows. They are set in regular rows divided by walkways running at right angles to the pyramids. The east-west pathway at the base of each pyramid gives access to both sides of the vines, and also serves as an irrigation channel. Our grapes are the juiciest and the sweetest in the world. We only pick them at peak ripeness for the finest flavor. The high quality also comes from the combination of eight to nine hours of sunshine a day, and the richness of earth they grow in. All of a sudden we spot one of our non-paying, illegal tenants who occupy the summerhouse in our absence. He is huge and magnificent in his, still thick and luxuriant, winter coat. It is a wolf. He steps out of the gaping entrance of the house standing for a moment with ears pointing, sniffing the air for danger he has sensed while still inside. He is poised for attack, or instant flight.

"Don't be frightened, children," says Mr. Gregorian, "he won't attack. Just don't make any sudden moves. His mate and cubs must still be inside, and he's protective of them. Just as your Papa and I would be under similar circumstances. He will try to draw us away from the house by making us chase him." True enough, the wolf gave another sniff and bolted into the bare rows of pyramid mounds.

"No, no. You can't go into the house," says Mr. Gregorian when we insist that we want to see the wolf cubs. "Father Wolf will be watching us, and Mother Wolf too. She will cover the cubs with her own body to keep them safe from harm. You wouldn't want me to shoot Papa and Mama Wolf would you, just so you can have a look at the little cubs?"

"No, no, Mr. Gregorian, please don't shoot them," we wail horrified, almost to the point of tears.

"Well then, let's go. I've seen enough to know what needs to be done here before you move in. Do you know," he added, "that wolves are very wise? Father Wolf has smelled danger, the smell of human beings. As soon as we have gone he will move his family to their summer lair, away from human habitation. Now that the snow is gone it won't be so cold up there."

Comforted by Mr. Gregorian's explanations, we come home to tell our story of the wise Papa Wolf, and Mama Wolf and her beautiful cubs.

I would like to think that wolves still roam the mountains of Maragha, rearing their young as they had always done. Unfortunately, it is not the case. Wolves have long gone from there, as have the children who joyously mimicked their lonely howling that echoed in the mountains on cool moonlit nights. As for THE Coral Snake, it disappeared about the same time this story ends, though he continues to live in local legends. He still wears his jeweled crown and holds court in his vast underground domain. It is also said he will return one day when human beings have learned to share their habitat with all the other creatures of the earth.

# 26

## A New Beginning

It is August and we have been on the mountain for two months. We are enjoying the long summer days and freedom from the high garden walls and barred gates guarded by that "monster" gatekeeper, Davoud. We roam freely over the property, play hide and seek among the vine pyramids, and ball games on the varazan. To cool off we swim in the stream, and occasionally dare to venture into the forest, the sinister abode of the banshee Desha Bakhtati.

Aunt Serunian and three of her children are taking their holidays with us, and Patroos is home from boarding school in Tabriz. Of course, where there is Cousin Patroos there is Cousin Hoosig. Those two always have their heads together planning some new mischief or outrageous amusement. The house is full of laughter. Papa's is the most infectious. There is never a dull moment. The setting is ideal for all kinds of entertainment. The varazan is our stage, and the house, with its high, wide verandahs, makes perfect seating for the audience. Outside, the vine pyramids stand guard like soldiers in orderly ranks, marching, phalanx after phalanx into the distance. On their breasts, huge bunches of ripening grapes lie snugly like decorations pinned to the chests of the valiant.

Today, our parents are entertaining several friends visiting from Maragha. Mama is with the ladies on the verandah while Papa has taken the men hunting for wild duck. We children, full of good food, play lazily in the hot sun awaiting their return. It isn't long before we hear the horses' hoofbeats on the earth and run to the path at the side of the varazan to meet the hunting party. For a brief moment, as the grooms lead the horses away, there is happy pandemonium. Instantly, though, the mood shifts. There is a loud scream, then Willie is shouting, "Papa, snake, snake, The Coral

Snake!" Everyone stands motionless, petrified, as all eyes turn to Willie's pointing finger. Just a few feet away, curled near the top of a pyramid and within striking distance of Homer, is THE Coral Snake. It is very thick and bulging, still digesting its prey no doubt, and very agitated. It must have been awakened from its sleep in the sun by the thumping of so many running feet and hoofbeats. Hissing and spitting, it uncoils itself moving its rearing head rhythmically from side to side with an evil look in its small, beady eyes. It is definitely not beautiful to me in this moment.

"Stand still, Homer," Papa commands, knowing that with the least added provocation the snake will strike and Homer will die an agonizing death. There is only one thing Papa can do to save Homer, kill the snake. Afraid of the possible effects of scattered shot, or the unthinkable consequence of missing the moving target, Papa decides to use the butt end of his rifle to break the snake's back. He is carrying his prized rifle which he brought back from America. It has a special safety catch to prevent backfiring, so it is safe. Everyone freezes into a slack jawed silence as time proceeds in slow motion. All at once, the stillness is shattered by a loud explosion and we are enveloped by thick, acrid smoke. When the smoke clears, we see Papa bent over and holding his side. Blood is gushing through his fingers staining his white silk suit a bright crimson. Crimson blood and red coral snake rings will haunt me forever. Papa's pith helmet and the broken gun are lying in the dust at his feet. Homer is unharmed, and of the snake - there is no sign.

Papa was taken down the mountain to our Maragha home where he could get better care. We kept a constant vigil with him. A surgeon was summoned from Tabriz to attend him, but due to flooding there he arrived three days later. It was too late. Our dear Papa died of blood poisoning on the third day. He lay on his deathbed with a single tear on his face at the moment of death. Life would never be the same again for us. He, whose life mission had been healing the sick and saving lives, could not be saved. His body was taken to Tabriz to be buried in the family plot next to our eldest brother, William, who had died of whooping cough at the age of three. Mama followed Papa's hearse to Tabriz and we did not hear from her again

159

for nearly a year. Emotionally and physically exhausted by the shattering events, Mama collapsed after the funeral with a raging fever, then pneumonia set in. In her delerium she would constantly call out for Papa and each of her children. In more lucid moments she would attempt to dress herself and come searching for us.

Of that period I have little recollection. A thick veil seems to have shrouded everything in its impenetrable folds. All I can see when I look back is that the sky always threatened with menacing black clouds, and the sun never shone.

Though I never again returned to the varazan, nor did I ever want to, that scene is as clear and fresh in my mind as if it had happened only yesterday. The memory of it has lived with me and has been a part of me for nearly eighty years. It is so deeply ingrained that when I close my eyes I can still see it clearly in every detail. The image is etched in black and white, the only color being a splash of brilliant blood-red on Papa's suit, and the sunlit glint of red rings on the snake.

It was nine months, almost to the day, after the painful events that changed our lives so dramatically, that the six of us, accompanied by Pari Baji and Martha, set off by *phergoun*, covered wagon, in search of our beloved Mama. Agnes, Angel, and Bobby were innocently ignorant of the concept of "Mama" and "Papa." I had become their proxy mother, so fiercely protective and possessive that I was afraid to leave them for even a moment in case they, too, would be taken from me while my back was turned. Homer and I indulged them, and Willie spoiled them shamelessly.

Mama had driven the two-hour journey to a chai khana at the foot of the great Tabriz-Maragha pass and waited impatiently for our phergoun as it wound its way down the naked mountain road. It was a lively scene as we came to a halt in front of the road house. There were people wandering in and out of the teahouse, coaches arriving, coaches departing, carts, phaetons, donkeys, and general excitement as the innkeepers tried to speed departures to make room for new arrivals. We spotted Aunt Serunian and Cousin Stella among the meandering crowd. They were waving to us, but my heart sank as there was no sign of Mama. With them was a pale and frail looking woman who, dressed in black, was walking toward us with outstretched arms and tears streaming down her face. Homer yelled joyfully, "Mama. It's Mama!" as he and Willie ran into her arms. When she opened her arms to me I refused.

"No. You are not my Mama. My Mama was pretty and she wore beautiful clothes." Tears were pouring down her face as she hugged and kissed the three little ones while kneeling on the ground. Then she looked up and called me "batee" (in the Assyrian language the word *bratee* means "my daughter" - *batee* is an endearing version of the word used with children.) The frost in my heart melted as I realized that she was, indeed, my mother. She had been the dearest, and most beloved mother in the whole world. As she wiped our tearstained faces with her soggy handkerchief, I looked skyward and noticed that the black clouds had lifted and the sun shone brightly – as if on a new life, a new beginning.

# Afterword

The Iranian nationalisation of the Anglo-Iranian Oil Company in 1951-1952, saw the breakup of our close-knit family circle. Homer, William, Agnes's husband Malcolm, and my husband George had been working successfully for the company in the refinery town of Abadan for some years. All four had good jobs, with the added security of generous retirement packages to look forward to at the end of their working careers. With nationalization of oil, everything changed. Mohammed Mossadegh was prime minister and the Ayatollah Khomeini, long quiet and low key while exiled in France, was beginning to stir. With the threat of Khomeini's imminent return to Iran, and his sworn vengeance on the Shah and all he stood for - modernism, cooperation with the West, women's emancipation, and the curtailment of religious power - the Shah's throne stood on shaky ground. For the second time in the twentieth century the thoughts of Iranians turned toward a republic, an Islamic republic, with the Ayatollah Khomeini at its helm.

Under these circumstances many Iranians, Christian as well as Muslim, saw no secure future in Iran and decided to leave. Some left to settle in the U.K., and many others to the U.S. Among the latter were my brothers and sisters with their families. Robert (Bobby), the youngest, was already working for the government in Washington, D.C. William with his wife Rubina, daughter Almira, and Mama moved to Florida. Agnes, a U. S. citizen like the rest of us, settled in Chicago with her husband Malcolm and daughters Hilda and Carol. My youngest sister Angel, with her husband Vartan and two sons Eric and Alvin, chose New York City. They gradually transferred their business interests out of Iran. Homer did not want to make the move at that time. He loved his lifestyle in Iran and wanted to stay since he had been offered a new and exciting job in Tehran.

I had been in England for several months when my husband George was able to join me in October of 1951. He, and many other employees, had stayed on the Iranian Oil Company's payroll for a number of months hoping that differences between Iran and England would be resolved. They thought that the British would be asked to return and continue their involvement in the oil industry. Unfortunately, negotiations failed shattering our hopes of returning home. In the meantime, the company did everything in its power to find alternative employment for those willing to relocate, or who wanted out. That is how George and I, along with our little daughter Angela, found ourselves traveling first class on the Orient liner *Orontes* bound for the antipodes, Australia! Ever since that long-ago occasion, and except for a little travel overseas, I have lived in Australia. In the process, I have acquired not only Australian citizenship, but several beautiful grandchildren and great-grandchildren.

In all those years of separation I missed my mother, brothers, and sisters terribly. I had not seen them since they made stopovers in England enroute to the United States. I was unable to see my dear Mama before her death in the U.S. in 1967. My husband George, also unwell, followed her in death some months later. In July of 1978, however, my plans and dreams materialized, and I was on a plane bound for Sydney, the first stopover on my voyage to visit my beloved siblings. I could hardly wait to see them.

On the flight my thoughts turned repeatedly to a night in wartime Iran. The whole family turned out to bid Bobby an emotional goodbye as he was quietly smuggled out of Iran to study in the U.S. What a cloak and dagger affair it was. All of Mama's efforts to get him out of the country legally had failed. There were two problems; our family had dual citizenship with Iran and the U.S., and Bobby was of conscription age for the Iranian National Army. The Iranian authorities were determined not to let him go to the other side. Bobby was just as determined to avoid Iranian conscription to not jeopardize his U.S. citizenship by swearing military allegiance to a foreign power. The U.S. Navy, with its wartime presence in the Persian Gulf, also showed a keen interest in my young brother's fate. They were just as determined to have him as the Iranians were. One could hardly wish to be more popular!

Arrangements for Bobby's departure were necessarily kept secret to not arouse the suspicion of agents assigned to watch our every move. This was when my cousin Victor, a brother of Stella and Hoosig and an intelligence officer in the U.S. Army, became our most important ally. Victor enthusiastically volunteered to organize all departure details, allowing the rest of us to go about our normal daily lives above suspicion.

His time to leave finally arrived. It was a velvet black night with not a soul to be seen on the streets. In the normally well lit town of Abadan, this night the streets were in total darkness with not a single light illuminated, not even through a crack in tightly drawn curtains and blinds. Earlier in the evening air raid sirens repeatedly wailed their bleak warnings, striking terror into every heart. To this day, Abadan has been an important oil refinery town and a potential target located at the confluence of two mighty Biblical rivers, the Tigris and the Euphrates. Even if one incendiary bomb had found a direct hit on one of the hundreds of towering storage tanks of oil, aviation fuel, benzene, kerosene, or other flammable by-products of oil, most of city would have exploded into flames and come down as charred rubble.

The suspense was almost unbearable and the danger very real as we waited on the banks of the Shatt-al-Arab River, which was enveloped by thick fog. Although we could not see the river, we heard the gentle lapping of water washing against the shore. Would the battleship's landing boat ever arrive? Had Victor given them the correct instructions, and would they find our jetty in this total darkness? Were there sharp ears listening, and spying eyes watching our every move, ready to pounce and cart us all off to jail? Were they now informing the Germans that an American warship was a sitting duck in these comparatively confined waters of the Shatt-al-Arab? A muffled sound and a disembodied American voice suddenly came out of the utter darkness beneath our feet. "Bobby, Bobby, are you there? Time to go. Keep quiet now, hurry, hurry, and be careful about lights." One last quick hug all around and he was gone, invisible as soon as he stepped into that dark void. Lost to me until now. Very soon, I thought, I would find my baby brother again on another continent half a world away from the land of our birth, in the full sunshine of a Seattle summer's day.

Robert, at fifty-eight, is still handsome, distinguished and youthful. He has been a widower for several years and has devoted himself to raising his four children. My heart gave a lurch when I first saw my handsome nephews as each, in a different way, reminded me of our father. Robert and my niece Bonnie (Ashlyn) took me everywhere to see the sights in Seattle and across the border into Canada and beautiful Vancouver.

My next stop was Chicago. On the flight, my heart fluttered at the thought of a reunion with my sister Agnes, her husband Malcolm and their two daughters Hilda and Carol. I pictured Agnes as she had been, smart and beautiful, with an enchanting, dimpled smile. The caption under her graduation photo in her College Yearbook reads: "Agnes Yoseph, the Sweetest Flower of the Field." Would she have changed much? Would I recognize her after so many years?

The reunion was a happy one. There was so much to say, so much catching up to do. We fell over ourselves in a babble of languages; Assyrian, English, Armenian, Persian and Turkish. In between we roamed over the vast open spaces of the midwest having picnics and barbeques. It was a restful and relaxing time that I badly needed.

After Chicago I flew to Cleveland, Ohio. There I saw my brother Bill (Willie) and his wife Rubina and their three children Almira, David, and Raymond. When she married Bill at the age of twenty, Rubina embraced my mother and our entire family as her very own. We, just as we wholeheartedly, took her into our hearts. Her accidental death, several years later in a car accident, left us all bereft.

## Monte Christo's Grotto

It was just as exciting seeing Bill and Ruby as it had been seeing my other siblings. Entering their lovely home was like a homecoming for me. Mama had lived in this house for twenty years. From here, regularly every week, she penned her beautifully written, newsy letters. From her descriptions I knew the entire floorplan of the house, its decor and furnishings, where her room was and, of course, Monte Christo's Grotto. But first, I wanted to be alone for a while, to spend a few minutes in Mama's room. As I sat quietly with my eyes tightly shut, I could feel her presence and could almost see her sitting at her desk, writing, writing, writing. By and by, some of her serenity seeped into my aching heart. I felt revitalised and peaceful, a needed shift from the agony I had felt since that day several weeks ago when my beloved grand-daughter, Mandy, had met with her shocking, accidental death.

Afterward, I was drawn to a certain door in the house that made me announce, "That, of course, goes down to Monte Christo's Grotto." Bill and Ruby gave each other a surprised look and started to laugh. Our dear well-read and inventive mother! When Bill and Ruby had first bought the house they had remodeled part of the basement into a family and entertainment room. Mother had kept me fully informed about every stage of the construction process. "Finally," she had written me, "the carpet was laid down today. It is a lovely ruby red, and when the overhead fans are turned on, the chandeliers tinkle and chime like *bulbuls* (nightingales) singing in a Persian garden. It is so beautiful and peaceful. I sometimes come down for a quiet read and imagine this to be Monte Christo's Grotto, and I an invited guest."

From half a world away I had longed to see this room. I had another clairvoyant experience as I saw Mama quietly reading in a cozy armchair that Ruby later said had been her favorite.

Ruby's love of entertainment left me no time for sorrow. Every day she invited friends for luncheons, dinners, or theater parties. I discoverd that the famous Iranian generosity and hospitality had not diminished at all on this side of the world. I also noticed an uncharacteristic new gregariousness among men and women that hadn't existed before Reza Shah Pahlavi unleashed female emancipation on the unsuspecting Middle Eastern male! After centuries of subjugation to male whim, women had discovered freedom and were not going to waste a moment of it. In Iran Ayatollah Khomeini had reversed the process, but the djinn was now out of the bottle and on the loose. Would it be possible to cork it up again?

By now I was getting homesick for Australia, my sunburnt adopted country. But, there was one more stop to make, New York, New York. Sister Angel was as elegant as ever. I noticed that after thirty years of marriage she and Vartan were just as devoted to each other as they had been when they first married. Their cordiality and warmth was touching, they wanted to keep me for always. Their house was my new home and there would be no arguments about it!

Angel and Vartan had two handsome sons, Eric and Alvin. Angel hosted a party for the newly married Eric and his wife Joy, inviting eighty or so guests. It was remarkable to see Eric and Alvin so grown up when only yesterday, it seemed, they had been toddlers.

Angel, a very confident and widely traveled person, took me on a tour of Washington, D.C. She showed me all the most important sights, the Washington and Lincoln Memorials, Washington's house on the Potomac, the Kennedy Center, and much more. We also took a guided tour of the White House, and visited Arlington Cemetary where our uncle, Lt. Colonel John Tamraz is buried.

I left Angel for a return trip to Chicago, a city of superlatives; the largest, the tallest, the grandest, and the stormiest. I came back to see Agnes and her family settled into a new home since my first visit. The house was lovely, with beautiful Persian carpets on the floor and shiny, oriental brass and silverware on display. Unfortunately, my dear sister did not live long enough to fully enjoy her new home. She died of leukemia on December 28, 1990.

Criss-crossing back to New York, on a day with the wind blowing up a blizzard all around us, Angel and Vartan put me on a plane to Boston, a connecting flight to London. Saying goodbye to all my loved ones across the States had been difficult, leaving me with mixed feelings on that return flight. I was sad to be leaving behind so many loved ones that I may never see again, yet happy to be going back home to my own daughter Angela and her brood in Australia. I was also downhearted that I would not be seeing my brother Homer who was still in Tehran.

As other Iranian expatriates, I watched Iran's headlong plunge into the dark ages and never had another opportunity to see my dear brother again. He who had led me into so much mischief, and so many fantastic adventures of fact and fiction, died of a heart attack in May of 1987, twenty years to the day of Mama's death in 1967. Homer adored Mama. Upon her death he inherited her role as head of the family, and her habit of writing to us every Sunday. For twenty years his letters, just like Mama's, arrived like clockwork, whether we answered him promptly or not. I miss my Knight in Shining Armor and his thoughtful letters.

At the airport in Perth I felt such a deep sense of homecoming, of belonging, especially when an airport official checking my papers smiled at me and said, "Welcome home, Mrs. Campbell, it is always nice to be home again, isn't it?" I looked up and saw my granddaughter Stacey running toward me with outstretched arms. Angela was following right behind. We all hugged and kissed with great emotion. It had been eight months since we had seen each other.